PENGUIN BOOKS

UK | USA | Canada | Ireland | Australia
India | New Zealand | South Africa | China

Penguin is part of the Penguin Random House group of companies
whose addresses can be found at global.penguinrandomhouse.com

First published by Penguin Books in 2020

Cover design and all illustrations by Andrew Weldon
Cover design © Penguin Random House Australia Pty Ltd
Internal design and typesetting by Midland Typesetters, Australia

Printed and bound in Australia by Griffin Press, part of Ovato, an accredited
ISO AS/NZS 14001 Environmental Management Systems printer

 A catalogue record for this
book is available from the
National Library of Australia

ISBN 978 1 76089 908 0

penguin.com.au

'Obey your leaders and submit to them.'
Hebrews 13:17

'I put my pants on first, shoes on second;
that's my sort of dress rule of a morning.
I find that helpful.'
Scott John Morrison

"I did it!"

August 24th 2018

I did it! Everything I have ever done has been leading to this point, and I finally did it! As of today, I, Scott Morrison, have become manager of one of the world's pre-eminent marketing firms: the Australian Federal Government. I know in my heart that I am destined to be the greatest leader this company has ever seen, and so here I present to you, dear reader, my diary. May it inspire younger generations towards the greatness I am destined to achieve and act as a blueprint for future leaders long after I have moved into the private sector.

Before we get to all that, though, I guess you need to know a bit about who I was before I became the boss. My humble beginnings. As far back as I can remember, I always wanted to be an ad man. It was a toss-up between that and being a priest, but I decided on the former because it offered greater variety in the things I got to sell. I had my first taste of the life as a child actor in my youth when I did a commercial for cough drops. There were a lot of great people on that film set, but the ones I looked up to most were the advertising executives. They drank whiskey, smoked cigarettes and had houses in the Shire – Sydney's crown jewel. They commanded so much respect that people would literally stop talking when they approached and stand there staring, obviously paralysed with admiration. When they weren't around, 'those f**king ad men' were all anyone could talk about, often tinged with the jealousy that comes with only being able to afford one car. After I graduated university I tried to track a few of them down, but the

ME →

AD DUDES ↵

majority had died. The few who hadn't were said to be in rehab, but I didn't want to bother them. I heard through the grapevine a few years later that they had also died. I like to think their legacy was giving a little boy named Scott a dream that would lead to him, years later, also owning a house in the Shire.

My acting career came to an early end when I auditioned for a part in a planned revival of *Skippy the Bush Kangaroo*. When I met the kangaroo playing Skippy, the animal panicked and threw itself in front of a passing truck. Its handler, understandably upset, said some pretty mean things about Skippy being able to 'sense great darkness within the child', and he later kidnapped me and tried to stab me with seven daggers on the altar of a local church. It was quite the kerfuffle. Afterwards, my parents said I was banned from working in an industry so full of drugs, perverts and loose morals, so instead I began my career in the more wholesome fields of marketing and politics. These two fields are essentially the same, except politics has the added bonus of being able to crush a weaker opponent, which adds a sense of victory to the whole thing.

After school I turned my focus towards crafting a personality for myself, slowly becoming the kind of leader with enough universal appeal to one day beat out a man with no eyebrows in a leadership spill. I adopted the name 'Scomo' when I noticed how popular a pop singer by the name of JLo (short for Jott Lorrison) had become. After several months I decided that velour tracksuits maybe didn't suit me as much as they did her, but the name stuck.

I spent some time in charge of Tourism Australia, left Tourism Australia by choice without being fired or ever called a 'smug f**king turd' by anyone I worked with, and finally, in 2007, I was offered a chance at preselection for the Division of Cook. I couldn't believe my luck! Not only was the electorate named after one of the very first Australians, it was also located in the greatest local government area on the planet: the Shire! My friend and mentor Bruce Baird was retiring as member for the area and suggested I throw my hat in the ring as a candidate. The only person standing in my way was a man named Michael Towke. Towke was an engineer, a former Army Reservist and, unfortunately for me, somehow very popular despite being a Lebanese candidate for a division that covers Cronulla Beach. He narrowly defeated me in the first round, 82 votes to 8. I was understandably furious at Bruce for embarrassing me, but all was not lost, it seemed, as some stories appeared in the media insinuating that Towke was a liar and that elements of his CV had been exaggerated. He was disendorsed by the party and I easily won the second ballot. I was going to be an MP! The rumours about Towke were later proven to be false and his name was cleared, but I think I was the right man for the job, so all's well that ends well. Now that I had preselection, all I needed to do was win the election, and I did that quite convincingly. Sure, the party may have suffered some losses, including the Prime Minister losing his seat, but the Shire got right behind me and I only suffered a swing of around 7 per cent against me, something described by others in the party as 'baffling'. Such are the wonders of miracles. Shout-out to my Guy in the Sky, the G-Man (God).

Six short years of opposition later, my good friend Tony Abbott led the party to victory over the Rudd–Gillard–Rudd government. Tony, an unnervingly muscular man who looks a bit like a fish if you taught it to ride a bike then poured a

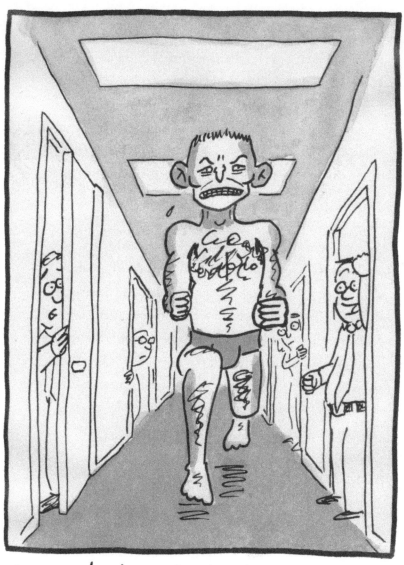

"...regularly stripping down to practise his slow-motion Baywatch run along the corridors of Parliament House."

lot of wine into it, discovered the power of the word 'no'. By simply saying 'no' and attempting to block everything Labor wanted to do, their popularity plummeted and, in turn, ours went up. It was a strategy he employed to great success, even while in power, until he didn't anymore when he was replaced as Prime Minister by Malcolm Turnbull after two years of not really doing anything other than regularly stripping down to practise his slow-motion *Baywatch* run along the corridors of Parliament House.

It was under Tony, though, that I was made Minister for Immigration and came up with what is still, to this day, one of my greatest campaigns: Operation Sovereign Borders. OSB was a multiplatform campaign that combined billboards and television commercials in multiple languages, on-water pop-ups courtesy of the Australian Navy, and offshore installations. My crowning achievement, however, was merging Customs and Immigration and rebranding them as BORDER FORCE!™ Unfortunately I was told there wasn't room in the BORDER FORCE!™ budget to have members of the agency surgically modified to replace their arms with machine guns, but this is the only thing I would have changed. In the years since I have

6

left the Immigration portfolio, it appears the name of the agency has been changed to mostly lower-case letters and the exclamation point has been removed, which, in my opinion, is far less cool.

I still keep a small memento of this campaign on my desk – a trophy made for me by a friend after he heard me complaining about not being allowed to enter my campaign at Cannes. It's a silver boat with the words 'I stopped these' printed on the side. The boat represents the boats that I stopped, and the message on the side is a reminder that I stopped the boats. Sometimes when I need to remember that the boats were stopped by me, I will look at this boat statue with the words 'I stopped these' on the side and think to myself, *I stopped the boats.* If I need to be reminded while I'm at home, I have a picture of the trophy on my phone and another in a frame in my study, or I'll have my receptionist go into the office and set up a video chat. I don't like to bother her when she's at home though, as she has a family to look after, so I'll only ask her to do this – at most – three times a week.

After I stopped the boats I had a brief vacation as Minister for Social Services before Malcolm decided my talents were needed elsewhere and asked if I would mind stopping the budget deficit as well. This proved slightly more of a challenge, since all that boat-stopping had cost quite a lot of money. The obvious solution was to cut welfare, but this would increase the number of desperate and impoverished people in Australia, which my boat-stopping campaign had been specifically designed to prevent.

Then I remembered a lesson I'd learned from my old friend Tony. After Malcolm beat him in the spill, Tony held a party in his office. The next day, when I asked one of the cleaners at Parliament House to vacuum up my Dorito crumbs, I was told he couldn't do it because he was 'still cleaning up the mess left by the former PM'. It was true that Tony's office was a reeking nightmare of urine, blood and other unidentifiable fluids, but as I watched him from the air vent, I realised he wasn't doing anything to rectify the situation. He had closed the door and was sitting amongst the detritus, playing a video game about angry birds on his phone. (I believe the game is called Angry Bird.)

I watched the man do this for several hours before I was struck by an idea. If I could somehow wallow in the mess the Labor Party's budgets had made of John Howard's beautiful, shiny surplus, I could coast through however many years it took for me to be given a new portfolio. The fact that we'd already been in power for a full term by this point would normally have posed a problem here, but luckily for me Tony had spent his entire time as PM continuing to talk about Labor. All I had to do was sit in my office, play Angry Bird and wait for my next assignment.

On April 21st 2018, after almost three years of Angry Bird, Malcolm called for the tri-yearly leadership spill, traditionally held towards the end of the first term of each Prime Minister since Kevin Rudd. Peter Dutton, the man who took over as the leader of BORDER FORCE!™ after I became Treasurer, had been canvassing for votes and had planned to move against Turnbull as soon as he had the numbers. I had been eagerly awaiting this moment too, although I could never say it publicly.

My plan was to let Dutton have the top job for a year or two, allow him to build up a large amount of resentment by looking like a hateful mushroom, then move against him and take the job for myself, picking up a nice popularity boost along the way. By allowing myself to be compared to Dutton, my possession of a soul would be seen as a positive attribute.

Malcolm found out about Dutton's ambitions, though, and called the spill before Peter had the numbers. Not wanting to reveal myself, I was forced to vote to keep things the way they were. I had thought that would be the end of it, but, as the plaque on Peter's office door says, 'How do you kill that which cannot die?' Even after his loss, that munted spud continued to gather supporters for another challenge.

This morning, just three days after the first spill, Malcolm stepped aside, declared the leadership vacant and said he wouldn't be running. My plan was back in action! Dutton could sail to victory unopposed, herald the beginning of the Apocalypse then be slain like the dragon he is by Saint Scott of the Shire! Everything was progressing exactly as it was meant to before frigging Julie Bishop put her hand up to run. The chances of a lady being voted in as leader of the Liberal Party were slim, but I still couldn't risk it. My plan would need to be accelerated. In the first round Dutton pulled in 38 votes, I got 36 and Bishop only ended up with a measly 11. Serves her right. She was eliminated and, in a case of history repeating itself, the second vote delivered me a victory with the final numbers being 45 to 40.

I haven't asked around yet, but I'm assuming a lot of the boys voted for Dutton to wind me up. We often play pranks on each other around Parliament House, like the time Christopher Pyne glued the windows and doors to my office shut and fed a pipe connected to his car's exhaust through the air vent. I was banging on the windows, begging him to turn the engine off, but he just cackled and did that thing where he spins his head around 360 degrees. Eventually Joe Hockey broke the door down and we were able to get Christopher back into his cupboard, but these japes were a regular occurrence around the old PH (Parliament House, not Pauline Hanson – Pauline hates jokes, says she doesn't get them). So all the guys voting for Peter as a joke is *definitely* something they would do. Accounting for prank votes, I put my real numbers at around 84 to me and 1 to Dutton. Josh Frydenberg was voted in as deputy, but no one really cares about that. He did vote for me though, so that was nice. Maybe I'll make him Treasurer as a reward. Hopefully he has a lot of games on his phone to keep him busy.

After the spill it was off to Government House to be sworn in. When we got there we were met by the leader of the National Party, whose name I can't remember right now, and his deputy, Bridget. They're nice enough but, honestly, people from the country are kind of strange. They have rough hands and smell faintly of soil and Bundaberg rum. Bridget also likes to wear her hair very high, like a cassowary, which is quite unnerving, but I feel like if I can get past being afraid of her we could work well together.

At the ceremony, I noticed Josh's Bible was written in a different language. I asked him what that was about and he said it's because he's Jewish, which is apparently just like Christian but with all the Jesus bits cut out, and you're not allowed shellfish. It still has all the cool bits of the Bible where God smites people, but I'm not sure I'd be much of a marketing manager if I was banned from eating lobster. When it was my turn to be sworn in, my advisors told me not to do my speaking in tongues bit when I laid my hand on the Bible. I still went 'balalalalalala' under my breath, but if I'm honest, not getting to do it at full volume made the ceremony a little underwhelming. All in all, though, it was a very good day.

August 25th 2018

My very first day as boss! I don't have a cabinet yet, so today I took a bit of me time. I started the day by spending two hours on the toilet going through YouTube on my phone. I found a very funny video of a Chinese man doing a horse dance and singing a song called 'Gumnum Styles' and sent it around as a group email to everyone at Parliament House. Jenny and the girls were a bit annoyed that I'd made them late for work and school by taking up the bathroom, but I told them that all the excitement of the previous day had made me severely constipated. They bought it. In actuality, I am incredibly regular, sometimes unfortunately so. To make sure they weren't too mad about not being able to take their morning showers, I made breakfast. I may be the world's most successful marketing executive, but I'm also a great dad. They had already eaten by the time I'd finished on YouTube, and they told me scrambled eggs weren't meant to include the shells but they appreciated the effort.

After breakfast I headed into the office for a very important phone call with a man I greatly admire. I have been a fan of Donald Trump since he began his career as a humble television judge on a program called *The Apprentice*.

Two teams would compete in a number of challenges to determine who was the best at selling hot dogs or cleaning fluid, and each week Trump would dismiss the worst contestant with his catchphrase, 'You are sacked!' I saw Malcolm walking past my office with a box of his possessions and called him in so Donald could hit him with the signature line. It's obviously been a while since he was on the show, so he messed it up a little and said, 'You're fired,' but Malcolm still got the message. He called me a shitweasel and stormed out. It was quite unbecoming of a former leader, and Donald and I had a great laugh about it.

Back when Turnbull was in charge, Trump's press secretary famously got his name wrong and referred to him as 'Trumble'. Well, Donald must respect me a lot more than that because he didn't get my name wrong once. In fact, he skipped right past calling me Scott or Prime Minister Morrison and only referred to me as 'Pal' or 'Buddy', which really drives home how quickly we have become friends. I told him about a couple of Australian heroes, like Bull Allen, an Anzac who was awarded a Silver Star by the US in World War II, and the Solo Man, who was the face of one of the most successful advertising campaigns the Australian soft drinks industry has ever seen. Trump was enthralled, hardly saying a single word while we spoke, except to ask his aide to order him a bucket of chicken for his dinner. We spoke for a full half hour, and I reckon we could have gone on for a lot longer, but the line cut out just after he said his food had arrived. I blame the NBN. Bloody Labor . . .

I also had a phone call with the Indonesian President, Joko Widodo, today. I asked him if they have Pizza Hut in Indonesia, and he said that, yes, they do, which I found fascinating.

I am about to sit down with the leader of the National Party, my new deputy – I think his name is Francis, or Stephen maybe – and hash out who gets what position in my ministry. MPs and senators have been trying to corner me all day in order to worm their way into my good graces. It's quite the change from when I was in school and would be picked last on every sports team because the other children were afraid that I'd outshine them.

August 26th 2018

Today, I presented my very first cabinet to the world! My Justice League!

First up, I had to find someone to take over Frydenberg's old portfolio of Energy and Environment. The dual portfolio was created under Turnbull when we all realised that the two go together perfectly. How do we create energy? Coal. And where does coal come from? The environment. Bunging the two things together was a no-brainer.

NEW MINISTRIES ?
MINISTER FOR PUBLIC SEATING
MINISTER FOR MINISTERS
MINISTER FOR NATURE STRIPS
There are so many!
MINISTER FOR MILK BARS
Protecting our heritage.
MILK BAR
MINISTER FOR CHEESE
MINISTER FOR VIDEO ON DEMAND
Fancy name for Netflix, etc.
MINISTER FOR GYMS, PERSONAL TRAINERS AND FITNESS CONSULTANTS
PUFF PUFF
MINISTER FOR SOUVENIRS
Approved varieties, standards, spell checks.
MINISTER FOR GENERATING BUZZ
I'll take this one.

Angus Taylor had previously been Minister for Cybersecurity, a portfolio I'd deemed unnecessary after seeing the NBN. Anyone trying to hack our databases would be dead from old age before they managed to download anything of any importance. Taylor sent me a message on Facebook asking for the position, and I had to admire his ambition. Before this I had been thinking of making him Minister for Families, since, with Kevin Andrews looking more and more like a vampire by the day, he was the person in parliament who looked the most like the father from a 1950s sitcom. However, I also needed a Minister for Energy, and what is more energetic than asking for what you want? I wrote back straightaway, 'Fantastic. Great move. Well done, Angus,' and gave him the job. I decided to strip out the 'Environment' part, though, when I remembered a story about Angus and some native grass from a few years ago.

Environment went instead to Melissa Price, because what is a Justice League without a lady one.

With Angus out of the picture for Families and Social Services I needed to find someone else. I decided to hand it to Paul Fletcher. Back when I won my preselection, I beat quite a number of young hopefuls. One of them was a man named Paul Fletcher. I wanted everyone to know that even though I had ground Paul into the dust all those years ago, I was a gracious winner and that there's no shame in a silver medal if the man with the gold is Usain Bolt. So I threw Paul a bone from the table as a show of goodwill.

Mathias Cormann told me he wanted to stay on as Finance Minister, and while I have yet to confirm it I have a suspicion he's a cybernetic killing machine sent back through time, and I didn't want to make him angry so I let him keep the portfolio.

Bridget McKenzie, the deputy leader of the Nationals, wanted Sport. She said she was heavily involved in sport, and when I asked her which ones in particular she pulled out a gun. I gave her the ministry along with a bunch of country things and quickly excused myself. I found out later, after I'd changed into my emergency trousers, that she is a competitive shooter.

Giving away the Sport portfolio left Greg Hunt without anything to do. I felt bad for Greg since, for some unknown reason, everyone around Parliament House called him Yorick, which made him furious. I don't know why. Yorick Hunt sounds dignified and Shakespearean to me. I tried to give him something similar to Sport, so he ended up Minister for Health.

Christopher Pyne also acquired his ministry through fear. He crawled inside the walls of my office and kept whispering that if he didn't get made the 'Minister for War, Death and Destruction' he was going to come out when I wasn't looking and stab me. I tried the usual trick of burning sage to get him out, but he began to screech at such a loud volume that I could taste blood in the back of my throat. In the end I just gave in and made him Minister for Defence. I awarded Steve Ciobo the portfolio for Defence Industry as an aide-mémoire, because I've always thought he looked like Christopher, if Christopher had managed to become a real boy and grow into an adult.

I made Dutton Minister for Home Affairs in the hope that he would take the title seriously and stay home. I walked in on him practising his smile in the bathroom mirror this morning and I'm not sure I'll be able to sleep much this month.

I picked Matthew Canavan as Minister for Resources because when I looked at every MP and senator we had, the one who seemed most suited to digging around in the dirt for lumps of coal was Matt. Plus, old whatshisface, my deputy, Brian somebody maybe, was getting a bit shirty that I hadn't picked many of his National Party mates for the plum jobs. I asked him if he'd like me to give a ministry to Barney Joyce and he shut up pretty quickly.

Kelly O'Dwyer, Karen Andrews and Marise Payne all got major ministries because my team told me I needed a few more lady ones.

At this point I was getting pretty tired and my deputy (his name might be Dean, actually) was really starting to get on my nerves, so for the rest of the spots I just pulled names out of a hat. Never be afraid to do this. Sometimes leaving major decisions up to God is the best thing you can do. Sure, I knew better than God for the ones I picked myself, but to claim I know better than Him on EVERY position would be nothing but arrogance.

I sent a message to Donald on Facebook Messenger to let him know what a great day I'd had announcing my squad and Messenger advised me that he had 'seen' it. I don't know many other people whose messages get 'seen' by the President of the United States. Do you? Great day.

August 28th 2018

Today my ministry was sworn in. I gave everyone a flag pin as a reminder of what country we represent. I got the idea from Sam Dastyari, who has a huge tattoo of the Chinese flag across his chest. My advisors said I probably couldn't force the entire cabinet to get inked, so I settled on the idea of badges. When they look in the mirror I want them to think, *Oh yeah! Australia! That's the one I'm in the parliament of.* Mirrors flip things though, so I had the badges printed in reverse so they'll be the right way round when they see their reflection. For the ministers without a reflection, I had them printed the right way round, since they would have no need to look in the mirror. I also avoided the use of silver, as I'm told those members of the cabinet are highly allergic.

August 30th 2018

Jenny and the girls said they want to spend this school holidays with 'people they enjoy talking to', which means my next chance for a family vacation won't be until the end of the year. That's months away! It's so unfair! I'd better get to go somewhere good. A tropical island somewhere maybe . . . All I can say is, if they're not going to let me take a holiday then I'm going to take A LOT of toilet breaks to go on my phone. Just like everything else in my life, if people refuse to give me the time off that I am owed then I'll just have to take it.

September 9th 2018

The first proper Newspoll since I became Prime Minister and it seems that Malcolm's final dig is making sure the public's hatred of him has transferred onto the party. The poll results that came out on the 26th of August don't count because I'd only just become PM, so they should not be looked up on Google. The LNP is currently trailing the ALP 44 to 56, but the main thing to look at is that my approval rating is up to 42 against Bill Shorten's paltry 36, which is a great victory for me personally. Before I replaced him, Malcolm was only on 44 to Bill's 32, and he'd had heaps of time to get to that point, so imagine how much the people will love me by the time it gets high enough to call the election.

September 10ᵗʰ 2018

Today was my first sitting day as boss and all the opposition wanted to talk about was Turnbull. Why did we get rid of him? Why did people say they supported him then sign Peter's letter to call another spill? All I heard all day long in Question Time was how great Malcolm is at this or how wonderful Malcolm did that. Malcolm, Malcolm, Malcolm! I'm sick of living in his shadow. I got rid of him weeks ago! Can we just move on, please? I'm in charge now, how about some questions about me, for once? Besides, as if I'm going to take leadership advice from Bill Shorten.

They also went on and on about Dutton's au pair thing, telling me to sack him. So he let a few au pairs without visas into the country, who cares? They were from Europe – the bits you go on holiday to, not one of the gross parts! What a waste of a firing that would be, like paying a parking fine with gold bullion. No, Dutton's sacking will be for something much bigger than this. I'm not sure what the scandal will be yet, but when it happens, me letting go of one of my high-profile cabinet ministers will look like the ultimate act of contrition. Little do they know that it will also be the best day of my life. He will finally be punished for taking the exclamation point off BORDER FORCE!

Some of the cabinet weren't wearing their special flag badges. I know it's just a good-natured joke and it's not coming from a bad place, but I didn't find it very funny.

September 11th 2018

Lest we never forget. Today is a reminder of just how much traction a leader can get out of something horrible happening. I wish I could preside over some sort of terrible event. Not one where anyone gets injured or dies. I don't want an actual terrorist attack or an epidemic of some new, deadly virus or anything – that would be far too much to deal with – but still something quite upsetting to the general public, like a statue of Captain Cook being knocked over or having paint splashed on it, maybe. An act of terrorism, but one that doesn't end up with anyone hurt or killed. Terrorism lite, if you will. Just enough to make a lot of people angry so I can placate them by denouncing it. Maybe then everyone would pay some attention to how great I am, and I could get on with the job of selling how fantastic our new government is. George Bush got so much great press out of his one, and he was way less popular and capable than I am. John Howard once told me that when he had dinner with Bush, the President wouldn't eat unless Dick Cheney pretended his spoon was an aeroplane.

Right now, everyone is distracted from the fact that I swept the floor with Dutton in the spill by the news that Dutton waved those couple of visaless floor-sweepers through immigration. I could not be more annoyed. To top it all off, he's having a very public spat with his former head of BORDER FORCE!, Roman Quaedvlieg. What did he expect? If you hire someone with a name like Roman Quaedvlieg to run your military squad, of course he's going to turn out to be your arch-nemesis. Has he never seen a James Bond film? I was actually shocked when I first saw a picture of Roman and he wasn't bald and stroking a cat. He's kind of a hunk, if I'm honest.

Maybe Roman is the James Bond and Peter is the villain. Although I have it on good authority that Dutton isn't allowed to own a cat since he got into a heated game of one-upmanship with the last one when it killed some native birds. Peter became an indoor minister shortly after.

Julia Banks has also been banging on about being bullied and is saying she won't be standing for re-election. I haven't even called an election yet, and as if anyone would bother to bully a quitter like her. I think she's just jealous of our cool badges. I ought to have Matt Canavan give her one of his signature atomic wedgies as punishment.

September 12th 2018

I finally cracked it at Bill today. For the third day in a row he kept asking me why I replaced Turnbull. Why do you think, Bill? Because I'm better than him! If the Australian people were so desperate to have him as their leader, why did he lose so many Newspolls? They hated Turnbull so much that even after I replaced him the Coalition lost another one.

"...a heated game of one-upmanship..."

I was prepared for another day of Shorten's nonsense, so before work this morning I gathered my bitchiest aides and we brainstormed some comebacks. I was in favour of, 'Talk to the hand, 'cause the face don't want to hear it,' or doing a rude finger and saying, 'Sit on it and rotate,' but in the end we decided on 'Get over it!' I have to admit I was a little disappointed I didn't get to incorporate a rude finger, but my team reminded me that there are cameras in the chamber and, even if I did look like a total badass, some of the older Liberal voters might be offended. We are heavily relying on them to elect us again before they die and we're left to deal with a bunch of kids who are afraid of the ice caps being completely melted by the time they're in their fifties.

I did see Bill in the corridor afterwards, though, and did that thing where you pretend you're winding your middle finger up and then down. He looked very upset and said, 'Is that really the sort of fing a Prime Minister does?' To which I replied, 'I guess it is, because I'm the Prime Minister and I'm doing it.' He scurried away with his tail between his legs and I got McDonald's for dinner to celebrate.

September 14th 2018
I need a holiday. I just got in trouble for a video an intern put on my Tweeter account. It was a fun little clip of me in the House of Reps making everyone put their hands

in the air, presumably like they just don't care, set to a small section of a rap song. I watched it before it was sent out and thought I looked suitably cool enough for it to be made public, so I gave the OK for it to be Tweetered. Unfortunately, although the title of the track was 'Be Faithful', the rest of the lyrics were anything but Christian. Unbeknownst to me, the song continues on to ask who is having sex that night, which I would never do in parliament, especially since our backbench includes George Christensen. That's an image that no amount of beers at the footy could scrub from my brain.

Once I found out, the video had to be taken down and the intern had to spend an hour coming up with an apology from me, time which could have been spent getting my lunch or shredding documents. It was such a waste of resources and something I should have seen coming. Apparently urban music can occasionally be vulgar, including references to 'bitches and hoes', and with everyone already saying we have a woman problem – even though my cabinet has SEVERAL lady ones in it – the last thing I need are racy lyrics played over a video of me getting serious work done. The only hoes I want are in the ads we run on rural television networks during the election. I'm pretty sure farmers still use hoes . . . I'll have to ask my deputy, David possibly, the leader of the National Party, when I see him next.

September 19ᵗʰ 2018

Finally got to let my marketing prowess shine in QT today. People have been going around sticking needles in strawberries for some reason, so it was up to me to save the strawberry industry with an award-worthy slogan. I hardly had to think about it. What food is a more iconic symbol of Australia (and/or New Zealand) than a pavlova? Aside from an Anzac biscuit, I mean. I settled on, 'Make a pav!' Short, snappy and to the point. Unless you top your pavlova with chocolate or exotic fruit like some sort of pervert, the making of one requires *strawberries*. If everyone makes a pav, everyone buys strawberries. If they make a pav every day, the industry is saved. Plus, as anyone who had a grandparent who didn't want to host Christmas but was forced to will tell you, people will eat a pav whether it has needles in it or not. They're just that delicious.

Bill also came up with a slogan: 'Cut the strawberries up, don't cut the farmers out.' What a bloated mess. It's no wonder he's stuck in opposition. First of all, who eats strawberries, or any fruit for that matter, by themselves? Fruit is a decoration or garnish for dessert. If I cut the strawberries up, then what am I meant to do with them? Secondly, that slogan is way too long. If I'm being driven down the highway in my Comcar and I see 'Cut the strawberries up, don't cut the farmers out' written on a billboard, I've got time to read maybe half of it. 'Cut the strawberries up' by itself just sounds vaguely menacing, and anyway, what is he doing talking about farmers? He's not in the National Party, so why would he care about people from the country? If anything, he should be supporting the people making the needles. Steel workers are unionised.

September 23rd 2018

The polls are starting to show how much I'm cutting through as Prime Minister. My personal approval rating is up to 45 and the LNP's two-party preferred rating is up two points! I believe that the success or failure of a party lies with the leader, so I am incredibly proud of this rise in our fortunes. This jump in the polls is proof to me that if the numbers were to go down again, it could only be someone else's fault.

September 25th 2018

Today I made an executive decision to refuse to talk about moving the date of Australia Day. I chose to address it today because we are exactly four months away from Australia Day, which I'm pretty sure is on January 25th, possibly the 24th. Whichever it is, it's a very important public holiday that dates all the way back to 1994, unless it's on a weekend, then the holiday is on the Monday. The specific date is so important because it's when Captain Cook first sailed into Sydney Cove in 1788 after a few days of killing animals and smashing up plants with a big stick around the corner at Botany Bay. It celebrates the founding of a penal colony that would go on to become the state that contains my beloved Shire, so you can imagine what it means to me. When Cook raised the Union Jack, a flag that would become the bit in the corner of the Australian flag, over that new British prison, he set in motion a series of events that would lead to the eventual creation of the great nation I now preside over as ruler.

Some people say we should celebrate Australia Day on the first day Australia became an actual country, but that's January 1st. New Year's Day, ever heard of it? Do you really want to waste a public holiday like that? I know I don't! Other people advocate for May 9th, the day in 1901 when we became a self-governing federation. I'd also like to point out it's pretty much in the middle of winter. Why would we want to move a summer holiday, where we can sit out in the sun and have a barbecue, for one in winter? What would a winter Australia Day even look like? You invite your friends over to sit inside and eat cold sausages and drink warm tins of beer, straight from the oven? No thanks! The Left's whinging has been getting louder and louder every year, though, so I needed a plan to put a stop to it once and for all. In typical Scomo fashion, I came up with a ripper.

What does everyone love more than a holiday? Two holidays! If people were so concerned about the date, why not have an Indigenous Day as well? I spoke with my management team and they said adding another national holiday to the year would put pressure on the economy and be a lot of work to organise, but I told them it wasn't a problem. Instead, I just launched a word-of-mouth teaser campaign. I did a tour of the country's most hard-hitting news providers – Seven, Nine, Sky, etc. – and told them all about my great idea. When they asked for specifics, I told them it was up to the states to decide and that we'd have a discussion. Anyone going back to talking about Australia Day instead of my new, hypothetical Indigenous Appreciation Day would be branded a racist for not wanting to respect Indigenous people. Job done!

'Having a discussion' is one of my favourite marketing tools. It's essentially the same as saying 'We should catch up' when you bump into an old acquaintance whose name you can't remember at the supermarket. Having a 'discussion' has no deadline, no required result and no finite length once it actually begins. If someone asks if you've made any progress, you can simply say, 'We are continuing to have that discussion,' and the person asking will have to accept that. An even better one to use is, 'I'm open to having a discussion when the time is right.' Theoretically, the time could never be right if you don't want it to be. Try using this the next time someone asks you to do something you have no interest in.

September 28th 2018

Jenny and the girls are still refusing to let me go on a holiday, even though I've said I'm happy for them to come along. My beloved Sharkies are out of the NRL finals, so I can't even enjoy the footy this weekend. Those bastards from Melbourne knocked us out last week, so I'm backing the Roosters in the grand final as revenge.

Of all the places I hate, I think I might hate Melbourne the most. They've got a Labor premier, the only federal Greens MP, Adam Bandt, comes from there and they follow AFL, which is the sporting equivalent of watching a herd of panicked gazelles run around an oval for two hours. Only in Melbourne, the snowflake capital of the world, would you get a point for missing a goal. It's also very popular in Perth, which makes sense when you realise that, at some point, every person from Perth will move to Melbourne then walk around telling everyone how big the sky is back home. The sky is big everywhere. You can just see more of it in Perth because there's nothing else there. The only thing Western Australia is good for is electing Liberals and digging iron out of, although, to be fair to them, they do give us about a quarter of our MPs and we do drag a lot of iron out of those holes.

WA – Plenty to go around!

October 3ʳᵈ 2018

Got in trouble today. I've only just found this out, but the former leader of the Nationals, the red one who likes to have sex, is called Barnaby. I've been calling him Barney for years! He's always answered to it, but today he was with his chief of staff and/or girlfriend and she kicked off and shouted, 'His name is Barnaby, you smirking fart in a jar!'

I didn't take her anger personally as being Barnaby's special friend must be incredibly stressful, but I apologised profusely. It's possible I've been embarrassing him for years and just haven't noticed him blushing because of his year-round sunburn, so I feel a little bit bad. It's important to keep on good terms with the Nationals since without them we couldn't form a majority government, and there's a reasonable chance that Barnaby will try to get his spot as my deputy back if something ever happens to . . . Ian? I think his name is Ian.

I've been racking my brain, trying to work out why I've been using the wrong name for Barnaby for so long, and I think I must have mixed him up with Barney Rubble from the *Flintstones* because of his tendency to wear a loincloth into parliament and hit things with a club.

October 5th 2018

Well, well, well. Guess who just topped the *Australian Financial Review*'s 'Overt Power List'. If you guessed me, then you would be correct. Because the answer is me! Overt. Power. Bill Shorten came in second, and I hope the shame of that silver medal burns inside of him until the end of time.

That turd Malcolm Turnbull didn't even rate a mention, even though he'd gone to the trouble of doing a photoshoot for it before the spill. In the pictures Malcolm is wearing nothing but his leather jacket and is posing very suggestively on a muscle car with the licence plate 'HOTDAD'. Apparently they were going to run the spread under his

catchphrase, 'I'm not like a regular PM, I'm a cool PM.'
I miss the old Turnbull, back when he felt like he belonged in
the Liberal Party, not the desperate Greens/Labor mash-up
he had to become to take the Prime Ministership off Tony.
The Malcolm I knew was a take-no-prisoners merchant
banker, decked out in the flashiest tuxedos and always ready
with a line that sounded like it came from a movie, like
'Humility is for saints,' or his personal favourite, 'Time is
money and I'm a motherf**king clock!'

He would often invite me into his office to try on his
extensive collection of top hats and monocles and have
money fights, followed by flagons of eighty-year-old cognac
and rare Dominican cigars in front of the open fire he'd had
installed. After the leather jacket arrived, though, everything
changed. Gone were the piles of hundred-dollar bills that
used to decorate his office, instead replaced with electric
guitars and copies of *Rolling Stones* magazine. He no longer
greeted you with 'Ahoy-hoy' and instead would ask, 'What's
up?' like some sort of tracksuit-wearing youth. Worst of
all, he flat-out refused to play Monopoly. Most people hate
Monopoly because of how long it takes to play, but Malcolm
could finish a game in under half an hour. Playing against
him meant certain defeat, but it was just a pleasure to watch
a master at work and especially fun if you could convince
someone who was unaware of his skill to join in. The look
on their faces when, 15 minutes into the game, Turnbull was

holding half the property on the board, all with two hotels, never stopped being funny to me.

I hope that some time in the wilderness will bring Malcolm to his senses and he'll realise the youth radio demographic are never going to love him like he wants them to. If he's so desperate to appeal to the younger generation, he's got a built-in fan base in the Young Liberals. Sure, they might be physically abominable lifelong virgins, but they're *our* physically abominable lifelong virgins.

October 6th 2018

I don't understand the Left's obsession with saving the whales. If I breathed air but still had to live in the ocean like a fish, I'd be *begging* for someone to harpoon me. Imagine being forced to swim even when you're asleep to stop yourself from drowning. No wonder they beach themselves – they're probably just trying to have a rest.

October 7th 2018

Finally, a chance for me to mix business and pleasure. The Premier of New South Wales, Gladys Berkjjkkijklijlkjn (please check spelling before publication), is facing pressure from the Left over her decision to let Racing NSW project a giant ad for a horse race on the side of the Opera House.

The Tweeters were furious and Change dot org, a website that has made a lot of money selling the Left the idea that they have some control over the world, had collected over 40,000 signatures protesting against it. Forty thousand sounds like quite a lot, but it's a lot less impressive when you realise it's less than one per cent of Sydney's total population, and the vast majority of those signatures probably came from Melbourne.

I've never been a huge fan of horseracing myself, but the ad men of my youth liked to watch it on the off chance they'd get to see a horse die, so I'm quite familiar with it. The objective is to menace and abuse a million-dollar thoroughbred until it is so afraid of a whip that the sight of it will cause it to run for its life, carrying a small goblin around a track in the process. The goblin clinging to the first horse to cross the finish line is then celebrated and, depending on its condition, the animal is either milked of its sperm or shot. Not a terribly interesting sport, granted, but you're allowed to get very drunk while watching it, so I can see why it's so popular in this country.

My interest in this situation wasn't to do with the sport, though – it was to do with the advertising component. For years I've looked at the Sydney Opera House and thought, *What a waste* . . . A shining white billboard in prime position on the city's waterfront, just *begging* to be adorned with a giant logo, instead left to decay, used only for

concerts and the occasional talk-show taping. I find it ironic that people are so opposed to advertising on an object that is itself the feature of so many tourism campaigns. I am often dismayed by how many great opportunities for advertising are missed simply because people don't want to 'deface historic monuments'. The pyramids, for example, would be the perfect place to install a four-sided triangular campaign, perhaps the new *Aladdin* movie, or something else that is popular in Egypt. Rugs maybe? I don't know, I've never been. Anywhere with that much sand and so few beaches isn't worth visiting, in my opinion.

I think my opinions on the matter are why Donald and I get along so well. He told me on our phone call about a deal he'd brokered to replace the Statue of Liberty's tablet and torch with a bucket of KFC and a drumstick, which I think is a genius move and one that is long overdue. With Donald's incredible success as a leader in mind, I decided to throw my Prime Ministerial weight behind Gladys. (This is not a reference to my actual weight. I am not fat. My shirt just puffs out sometimes and makes me look bigger than I am.)

Alan Jones also stepped in and did what he does best, getting irrationally angry on the radio and asking for someone (other than him) to be fired. Some people said that I shouldn't have gotten involved, as it was a state issue, but Australia is a federation of states. I firmly believe, as I have always believed and always will believe, state issues are federal issues. I might not tell them how to spend their budgets, but the big stuff? Stuff like public outcry and natural disasters? That is 100 per cent my responsibility as the leader of this country.

I look forward to this ad going ahead and setting the standard for heritage-listed monuments to be used as billboards. Just think of the budget surplus we'd have if we were allowed to sell ad space on the side of Uluru! We'd probably have to paint it white though.

October 8th 2018

I spent the morning talking to Alan Jones between ad breaks on his breakfast radio show. One thing that Alan brought up was nuclear power, which I do not have a problem with. It's been widely reported that I'm not a fan, but I just want to set the record straight once and for all: nuclear energy is fine, it's just that coal is better.

The first benefit of coal is that it's cheap. Why spend good money on uranium when you can get so much more coal for the same price? I remember taking Jenny to a fancy restaurant for our first wedding anniversary and being appalled when I saw how expensive the tiny portions were. All I could talk about the whole night was how many chips at McDonald's this money could be buying us, to the point that we had to leave before dessert because the other diners were starting to complain. Every anniversary since then has been spent at McDonald's, where I spend up big, ordering every item on the menu (except for the Filet-o-Fish, because that's disgusting). Think of coal as a supersized Big Mac meal with Fanta and a large strawberry sundae, and think of uranium as a single organic carrot. Both are technically food, both cost the same amount of money, but only one of them will leave you full enough that you're at risk of vomiting. Given the choice, I'll eat coal every time.

Another reason I prefer coal-fired power is that nuclear energy produces a large amount of waste. Since the UN put a ban on pouring radioactive waste into the sewers after the creation of the Ninja Turtles in the 1980s, the only thing that can be done with the barrels of toxic sludge is to bury them. This poses a problem though, as our economy relies on our ability to dig things up, and if there's a layer of barrels just beneath the surface of the earth, our efforts will be severely hindered. Burning coal, on the other hand, produces nothing but harmless CO2, which you can't see or taste, floats away by itself and is consumed by plants to make food for poor people and vegetarians.

Finally, there's the risk that comes with producing nuclear power. I once famously smuggled a piece of coal into parliament to perform a bit of prop comedy, much to the delight of the backbenchers and everyone watching at home. If this had been a piece of uranium, it might have been a lot harder for people to differentiate between me and Dutton in the spill as, like him, my eyebrows would have fallen out. Nuclear power plants are also much more likely to explode, leaving the surrounding area almost uninhabitable for years. George Christensen has spent a lot of time inside reactor 4 at Chernobyl, and according to him the surrounding area is nearly as bad as Western Sydney.

October 10th 2018

Back on 2GB chatting to Alan on his show today to announce that Australia would no longer be putting money into the UN's Green Climate Fund. We've been depositing cash into it since 2015 when – surprise, surprise – Malcolm signed us up to take part. Trust Turnbull to pledge money to something with the word 'green' in its name. That was typical for him back then, all 'I believe in climate change!' and wanting to pass legislation in his fancy leather jacket. Thankfully the party's powerbrokers were able to put a muzzle on him by reminding him his post-Prime Ministerial job in the private sector might not exist if his climate policy closed down the economy, and if there's one thing Malcolm enjoys more than being popular it's large amounts of money.

So in an attempt to help Josh out with his first budget, I decided we should pull out of the agreement. A lot of countries were upset, of course, especially the poor ones, which is typical of them. They're always complaining about some famine or plague, and the second you decide to put your budget in surplus instead of helping keep their people alive, they're up in arms. The main point of contention seems to be that if we don't slow climate change (if it even exists), then a lot of Pacific Islands will sink beneath the waves, never to be seen again. The loss of these islands will be sad, sure, but I have to think of the Australian economy, even if it means giving over some of my favourite holiday destinations to mighty Poseidon. I said this to Alan on his show and he frantically hit the dump button, which his producer told me is normally reserved for when Jones pulls out one of his jokes about Julia Gillard's dead father or starts reminiscing about the Cronulla riots. My media advisors later told me that, while true, my argument perhaps shouldn't be spoken out loud, so I'm writing it down here instead.

October 12th 2018

Today I threw the Labor Party a bone and agreed to support their idea that gay students shouldn't be expelled from private schools because of their sexuality. The initial plan to kick them out came from a Religious Freedom Review we had Philip Ruddock do. It was never supposed to see the light of day, much like Ruddock himself, lest he burst into flames, but he was bored and wanted something to do while he finished decomposing.

Now some of the more Old Testament-y recommendations have been leaked, and we're having to head them off with something I find even more revolting than the smell of Philip's crypt: progressive policy. It might not seem like something I'd normally do, because the Bible says homosexuals are an abomination, and being abominable should at least get you a suspension, but as my advisors pointed out, the same-sex marriage plebiscite showed that the majority of the country thinks they should be respected, and I'm not about to leave votes on the table. I'm sure God will understand. After all, he wouldn't have created gay people if I couldn't get votes off them.

October 13th 2018

It's a week until the by-election for Malcolm's old seat of Wentworth and things are looking a bit dicey. People still hate Turnbull so much that they're potentially going to vote against his replacement, Dave Sharma, who we picked because of the electorate's previous affinity for wealthy white men. Kerryn Phelps, the person they're shifting their vote to is, as far as I can tell, a woman who owns a single green jacket. I'm all for having more lady ones in parliament – I'm on the record as being a staunch feminist – but they have to be lady ones from the Liberal Party and they have to do what I say.

October 14th 2018

Another Newspoll, another bump in the numbers. We're up in the two-party preferred by another point, which puts us at 47-53. I can do no wrong! At this point, I'll eclipse Malcolm's last four Newspoll results of 49-51 in no time! I'm on track to have the best numbers since John Howard led the party (the second time, not the first).

October 16th 2018

Great. Just great. Mathias Cormann has led our senators to vote for a motion put forward by Pauline Hanson that

'It's OK to be white.' I mean, of course it's OK to be white – the vast majority of the LNP is Caucasian – but this specific phrase is, I'm told, associated with white supremacists, which is never a good look.

This is exactly why we never vote for anything Pauline puts up. It's like eating a cake made by an unsupervised three-year-old. Sure, it might look fine on the surface, but you just know they don't wash their hands after using the toilet, and there's a very good chance the cake has rocks in it.

The opposition and the crossbench voted it down, thank God, and I've had Mathias release a statement calling it an administrative error. On the plus side, it might help us win some of the white nationalist vote back from Pauline at the next election.

October 19th 2018

I am furious! Some little twerp has paid $50 for my website name and replaced my personal page with a song about a person having sex with a woman. The song itself doesn't really bother me. The lyrics are about a man with my name who is being cuckolded by the singer and his girlfriend, Fiona. My wife, Jenny, is obviously not called Fiona, so there's no way this song could be about me, and I had ASIO interrogate Jenny to make sure it wasn't a pseudonym.

What's really gotten my goat, though, is that my domain name was sold for such a measly sum. I am a world leader, the most overtly powerful man in Australia, and when whoever's job it was (not mine) forgot to renew my website name they sold it for $50?! Absolutely disgusting. For me, obviously, it should cost that much, because I refuse to pay anything more, but the value of it on the open market should be at least a million dollars.

In the past three weeks we've had over seventy unique visitors, and the price they put on that booming traffic is $50?! We've got the domain back now but Josh is going to have a much harder time getting the budget into surplus because of how much we had to pay for it.

October 20th 2018

Obviously people haven't forgotten how much they hate Turnbull, because that Phelps woman with the one green jacket just won the by-election, and now I'm stuck with one less vote on the floor. I've only got 75 out of 150 in the house now, meaning I have to convince an independent to vote with us if I want to get anything done, the result of which will be having to talk to Bob Katter.

I don't have a problem with Bob, although every time we try to secure his vote for a piece of legislation the only thing he'll ask for in return is that we stop his neighbours from being eaten by crocodiles. I've looked into it and the numbers don't appear to be especially high in his area, but Bob owns a gun, so whenever he brings it up I just smile and nod. I wish the division of Kennedy would elect a National so I didn't have to deal with him, but it's hard to get the electorate to vote for anyone other than Katter because every person who lives there is related to him by blood.

This is all Malcolm's fault. Why couldn't he have stayed on the backbench? I know I told him to get out and never darken parliament's door again, but he didn't have to listen! Tony Abbott didn't! At the very least he could have helped campaign for his replacement. I know it might have been demoralising, but how is it any more demoralising than being removed from office by Peter Dutton?

October 27th 2018

Someone at the Institute of Public Affairs isn't doing their job. According to the papers, they've 'blasted' my plan to bring down energy prices by breaking up the big power companies. This goes completely against the IPA's reason for being, which is to get Coalition governments elected and give jobs to members of the Young Liberals whose heads are too objectionable for us to employ them as staffers. I'm never going to actually break up the big power companies – they donate far too much money to the party – and the

IPA should know that, but people like to be told things are happening, even when they're not.

It's like being told to get up and get ready for school when you're a teenager. The later it gets, the more anxious your mother becomes that you won't be there before the first bell, but if you stick your leg out of the bed and stomp it around on the floor every now and then, she'll calm down and stop nagging you. Telling people, 'We're working on it,' is the same thing. It soothes them just long enough to elect you again, and then you've got another three years to relax and tread water before you have to think of something else to 'work on'.

October 28th 2018

The curse that is Malcolm Turnbull has struck again. Today's Newspoll has us back down to 46-54. Worse still is what the memory of Turnbull has done to my personal approval rating, which is also down a point. I am the leader and I accept responsibility for poll results 100 per cent, but some things are out of my control, like people thinking back to two months ago when they're asked their opinion of the government. I think it might be time to remind everyone just who the Prime Minister is with a big multiplatform campaign. Something impressive and flashy. Maybe a bus?

Jenny and the girls have been going on about wanting to see a movie called *Bohemia Rhapsody*, about the rock-and-roll band Queens, which has posters plastered across the side of every bus in Sydney. I'm not sure why they're so excited to see it. No judgement, but they've made the main character look a bit gay on the posters, which, for a movie about rock stars, cannot be what they were going for. Maybe if I was on the side of a bus, though, everyone would be talking about me. 'Let's go see the Scomo movie,' they'd say, before realising that it's on television every sitting day and it's called Question Time. Instead of seeing me gunning down aliens or karate kicking baddies off mountains, they'd see me owning Bill Shorten and telling great jokes that all my mates behind me laugh at.

A bus is the perfect advertising strategy since people get a bit funny if you start running campaign ads outside of an election, but if it's a form of transport I can simply claim it

as my personal vehicle, which I can decorate however I want. Even better, the bus could drive from city to city and I could pop out and surprise people!

I'll have my staff run the numbers.

November 5th 2018

My bus idea is going swimmingly. There wasn't a lot of money in the budget for the fleet of buses I'd hoped for, but we were able to afford one. I dubbed it the 'Scomo Express' and decided that, since we couldn't roll out the campaign Australia wide, we should send it to the one place in the country where people are still impressed by things going *vroom*: Queensland. There was also a bit of cash left over that went into buying the 'Bill Shorten is a Shifty Little Toad' moped, but so far this has received a lot less media attention.

I was beginning to second-guess my idea of actually being on the bus when I saw how long it was going to take to drive between cities up there, but then my team reminded me just how much air travel I can expense without getting in trouble. My plan is to use my private jet to go from place to place, then jump on the bus at the airport before getting off again to do my campaigning. Some of the whinier members of the Left have complained about this, but I have it on good authority that this is exactly what the beloved rock star Bob Jovi does, and he never had a country to run.

The bus is painted blue and has a big picture of my face on the side with the slogan 'A stronger economy, a secure future'. I got to come up with a bunch of slogans for this campaign, which I was thrilled about. Along with the main one we also have 'On the road to a stronger economy', which is a joke about how buses drive on the road, and 'Backing Queenslanders', which plays to their state pride.

For a state that gave us cane toads, skin cancer and Peter Dutton, Queenslanders are strangely very proud of where they live. Anyone who has ever watched a State of Origin rugby league game will be all too familiar with the guttural scream of 'Queenslander!' Not 'I am a Queenslander' or 'I'm proud to be a Queenslander', just 'Queenslander!' Like Tarzan if his mum and dad were siblings. I don't want to sound ungrateful though, because they elect us in droves. The only part of Queensland I don't like is Brisbane. It's full of artist types who walk around wearing jeans in the summer, talking about how backwards Queensland is until they eventually move to Melbourne, only to come home as soon as their first lease is up because 'there were too many Asians'.

Queensland.
Queensland
one day,
Queensland
the next.

QLD.

November 6th 2018

Labor will try anything to win the public back. A few days ago I released an online mixtape of my favourite songs on an internet page called Spotify, and what do you think Labor's response was? Do you think they thanked me for introducing them to a bunch of cool bands like Talking Head or U2? Of course they didn't, because all Labor is concerned with is point-scoring. They're so jealous of all the points I've scored against them that they're desperate to win some back. Unfortunately for them, I'm Peter Sampras and they are a tennis player who isn't as good as Peter Sampras.

Their main criticism was that there weren't any Australian artists on my mixtape, as if being Australian is more important than writing solid-gold hits like that 'I get knocked down' song about drinking whiskey drinks and singing other, better songs. Still, this outcry presented a great opportunity to score a point off Labor, so I gathered the top musical minds in my office and had them dig up a bunch of tracks by obscure Australian bands and add them to what is known as a 'play list'. They did not disappoint. Before I knew it, I had a play list filled with Australian music by little-known bands like Crowded House and Split Ends. My team asked if I wanted them to mix the artists up a bit so it didn't look like they had just gone artist to artist and added three or four songs by each one, but I decided against it. I thought it looked better grouped together as it showed that I didn't just know one hit song by, for example, the band In Excess, but was well versed enough in their music to know a number of their singles.

The response was fantastic and several people complimented me on it, including one staffer who said the play list had 'hella bangers' on it, which I'm told is not an insult. If I'm honest, it's nice to finally be recognised for my great taste in music.

November 7th 2018

I've come up with a new slogan, which has been getting a real workout during this bus/plane tour of Queensland: 'I'm listening, I'm hearing, I'm doing.' I think it could possibly be one of the best of my career. Like all good marketing slogans, when you really think about it, it doesn't actually mean anything, but that's what's so brilliant about it. You allow the consumer to assign their own meaning.

If your slogan has a fixed meaning, that's the only thing you can campaign on, but by leaving it open to interpretation, you could potentially be campaigning on issues you don't even know exist. The beauty of 'I'm listening, I'm hearing, I'm doing' is that it is all things to all people, which is widely known to be the best leadership style. The only definitive meaning it has is 'I am literally fixing every problem you have', much like Christopher Pyne's excellent 'I'm a fixer.' Although in Christopher's case, fixing has a much more sinister meaning. When angered, he will often say things like, 'If I have to fix you, they won't even find your bones,' before scuttling up into the ceiling to whisper swearwords at people.

November 8th 2018

Today I announced a $3 billion initiative to help with the building of infrastructure in Pacific nations. This morning my plane met the bus in Townsville, and if anything will have you thinking about elsewhere it's being in Townsville. This trip to Queensland has helped with my need for a holiday slightly, in that I got to sneak off to Wet'n'Wild when we were on the Gold Coast, but nothing beats the real thing. If I donate enough of Australia's money to places like Fiji and New Caledonia, maybe they'll invite me to stay for a week as a thank you. Jenny and the girls couldn't stop me from going because I'd technically be there on official business, but I could sit by the pool, drink beer and play as many games on my phone as I wanted. Hawaii is technically in the Pacific too, but I don't think even *I* could sell the idea of donating aid to the USA. Oh well. I'll get there one day.

Hopefully this also makes up for that time Peter Dutton was caught telling Abbott and me a joke about the future drowning of Pacific people while we waited for a meeting about refugees to begin. The joke was something along the lines of, 'Time doesn't matter when you have water lapping at your door,' and Tony dutifully did his strange, robotic laugh where he actually says the word 'Ha'. I remained unmoved though. Firstly, because Dutton has terrible comic timing and botched the punchline, and secondly, because I knew exactly what was hanging over our heads.

Peter apparently wasn't aware that the fluffy thing on a pole above us was a boom microphone, recording our every word. I let Tony get a few more of his 'Ha-Ha's out then dutifully told my then-leader that we were being recorded. Peter later told me that he had seen the boom but had thought someone had just killed a stray cat and was displaying it as a trophy. In hindsight, it is perhaps a little bit unfair to expect an ancient blood golem wearing a Queensland police officer as a suit to fully understand how technology works.

November 10th 2018

I've decided to become a hat guy. I got the idea when we
were up on the Gold Coast and I was trying to organise my
lunch break so it would line up with the Police Academy
Stunt Show at Warner Bros. Movie World, which is like
Hollywood but on the Gold Coast. One of my staffers came
up to me and said a lady had sent me a hat. I was about to
have it thrown away when he told me the lady in question
was Mick Fanning's mum, who he then went on to explain
is a famous surfer, making her famous by association. Not
wanting to pass up the opportunity, I donned the hat and
headed down to the beach to make a Tweeter video. I made
sure to mention a few times that the woman was Mick
Fanning's mum, so it didn't look like I was just wearing
a hat given to me by some boring, regular, non-famous
member of the public, chucked in a 'fair dinkum' to remind
people which country I'm the leader of and had my staffers
post it.

Watching the video back, though, I realised something:
wearing the hat made me look cool! I mean really cool,
like I was James Dean or Cliff Richard. I'd always liked my
friend Donald's hat, but I didn't think wearing the words
'Make America Great Again' on my head was an appropriate
thing for the Australian Prime Minister to do. Don't get
me wrong, it's definitely one of Australia's objectives on the
world stage, but we also have others, and 'Make America

Great Again and Also Sell a Lot of Coal to China and India' doesn't quite fit on a hat.

November 11th 2018

I think perhaps Newspoll is calling the wrong people. Today's result had the party down by another point at 45-55 and my personal approval down to 42 against Bill's 36. I mean, I'm still beating him of course – even if you fudged the numbers completely he's still Bill Shorten – but I find it hard to believe that it's only by six. I might get on the phone to Uncle Rupert later and ask him to start calling the right people to give a better indication of just how successful and popular I am. Perhaps I could provide him with some phone numbers from the Liberal Party's member database.

November 13th 2018

In Singapore for a couple of days for the ASEAN Summit. God, it's boring. No good beaches or anything. A complete waste of a trip. I think it really needs to be a rule that if you're going to have the most powerful people in the world fly into a country to conduct business, that country should, at the very least, be a tropical paradise. Jeffrey Epstein is one of the most evil men to ever walk the earth, a truly reprehensible person who is beyond even God's forgiveness, but when meeting with past and future American presidents, even he had the decency to put them up on a private tropical island.

November 17th 2018

In Papua New Guinea for a couple of days for another summit. I was actually really looking forward to this one because Trump was meant to be attending, but I got here to find out it's just Mike Pence. If I'd known that Donald wasn't going to turn up, I'd have sent my deputy too. I really need to learn his name. Maybe I should write it on my hand.

November 19th 2018

Mike Pence is a truly terrifying man. Before today, I had never felt physical pain from boredom and didn't think it was possible. After our meeting, though, I spent a good 30 minutes coughing up blood and the word 'Midwest' now causes me to involuntarily flinch.

November 22nd 2018

The lefties are up in arms again over some comments I made about immigration. All I said was that we should cut immigration because our roads are choked with cars and public transport is full. I got the idea when my comcar was stuck in traffic behind a truck on my way home. There was a bumper sticker on the back window with a picture of Australia and the words 'F**k off, we're full'. Simple, effective branding. I jumped on Google, found the sticker in question within an hour and ordered 20,000 of them with the office credit card. My plan was to launch a grassroots campaign with this slogan and hand the stickers out at events. My staff advised me that, even though I'd launched a tourism campaign with the slogan 'So where the bloody hell are you?', sensibilities had yet to change quite enough for me to run a slogan that included the words 'F**k off', even if the rudest letters were replaced with little stars. It was the same reason we had to cancel my follow-up ad, 'Visit Australia, d**khead!' For a country that loves to use the C word, something I hear on an almost daily basis, often used as a term of endearment as I leave the room, this country is still very averse to big swears being used in advertisements.

My staff were slightly worried about 20,000 unused stickers appearing on a parliamentary report, but the guys in the One Nation office took them off our hands. The sentiment of the sticker stuck (this is a clever joke about stickers sticking) with me though. People were angry enough about traffic and crowded buses to claim that a country that is ninety per cent uninhabited is full, and that's something that can be capitalised on. Re-education campaigns are tricky and often unsuccessful. If the amount of successful sex criminals in the music industry have anything to teach us, it's that people don't like to change their minds. The first rule of marketing is pander to people's fears, never challenge them.

Because of this clever bit of spin, though, the lefties on Tweeter are acting like I'm Peter Dutton or someone. I think maybe because I stopped the boats they believe that I'm a racist or anti-refugee, but that is simply not the case. Where a person comes from or how they come into our country doesn't bother me, but it bothers the voters we are chasing. I don't like vegetables, but you can bet your arse that if I was overseeing a major fresh produce account you'd see me biting into a head of broccoli at every media call. It's just good business. I mean, sure, personally I'd prefer a doctor from Syria who had to leave their country due to war over a British backpacker who's overstayed on his fruit-picking visa. Refugees, by and large, work hard to build new lives in the countries they're settled in because their old homes are likely gone forever. They're also far less prone to trying to sign you up to a charity while you're doing your shopping, but the Australian (Queensland) heart wants what it wants. It's like my friend Philip Ruddock once said to me as I was taking him in to get reupholstered, 'You either stop the boats or you stop the votes.' I think he also had an aversion to sea vessels in general, though, as it's widely known he can't travel over open water.

November 25th 2018

I don't know what Uncle Rupert's problem is. He's happy to run headlines supporting me and make sure his journalists only ask the questions we've asked them to, but his guys keep calling people who give the party bad Newspoll results. We should not, for the second poll in a row, be down 45-55. Especially when the Labor Party is being headed up by Bill Shorten, a man so forgettable that the facial recognition scanners at Parliament House don't work for him, requiring him to use a special key.

I need my holiday. We're about to head into another two full four-day sitting weeks before I get some time off for Christmas, and I am already exhausted. Jenny and the girls might push back on it, but I'm going to have to demand that I'm allowed to go to the beach for a week, even if it's just a boring local one.

November 27th 2018

Well, I guess that's a second Julia in Australian politics with a victim complex. First Julia Gillard did that speech about how Tony hates women (when his own wife IS ONE), and now Julia Banks has left the Liberal Party to sit on the crossbench because she thinks she's been 'bullied'. What else can you expect from someone from Melbourne, the city where riding a bike instead of driving a car is seen as a life choice instead of a sign of poverty and source of great shame. This little stunt took all the attention off my own announcement that Josh was going to deliver a surplus budget, which is infuriating.

Josh has been dragging his feet a bit on making cuts to social services, so I decided to put the wind up him, but now all that pressure is gone because all anyone can talk about is how some random Victorian who has been in parliament for all of two years doesn't like the fact that she's in a right-wing party. If she wanted to represent the centre-right she should have joined Labor. Craig Kelly also threatened to defect if he didn't get preselection next year, but I had a staffer send him a Slinky and he's been too distracted making it walk down the stairs to bring the matter up again.

November 30th 2018

I'm in Argentina – and Donald is here! I couldn't get a meeting scheduled with him because he's very busy, but I saw him at the 'class photo', where all the leaders stand together for a picture, and he made this hilarious joke where he pretended to think my name was Malcolm. I laughed and said, 'You know my name is Scott,' and he kept the joke going by saying, 'Who are you?' before his minders rudely interrupted our conversation and ushered him away. I went to talk to his friend Vladimir instead. He asked if I wanted some help with the next election, saying he'd done a lot for Donald's campaign. I assume he was offering to fly over and do some doorknocking, but I told him there was no need and explained to him who Bill Shorten was. I did ask him if he could get Trump's office to squeeze me into his schedule though, and he said he'd see what he could do.

December 1st 2018

Putin came through! He got me a fifteen-minute meeting with Donald when the President's office had been telling me he'd be too busy to even talk to me if I bumped into him in the corridor and not to try making conversation. We had a really good chat about why I'm in Argentina and Malcolm isn't, and I explained in great detail how I crushed him in the spill. It was quite similar to the conversation we'd had on the phone back when I first took office, but I assume Trump just loves the story so much that he wanted me to tell it again. I am, after all, known for my engaging speaking style. The press were present for the first couple of minutes of our meeting, and I wish I'd been able to have my full quarter hour in private, but this is how things are done in the big leagues.

As we were wrapping up, one of Donald's aides made a cheeky joke about needing to get to meetings with 'the real world leaders' and everyone laughed. The American sense of humour can be quite harsh if you're not used to it (I once had an American friend in university who would call me a 'worthless dweeb who will only ever achieve whatever success is handed to him'), but it's a cultural thing so it's polite to laugh. I've noticed this sort of humour creeping into Australia more and more in the last few years too. It's now quite a regular occurrence for someone to call me a 'fetid little toad' or 'junior vice-president of the marketing team' as a joke. I know it's harmless teasing and would never take it to heart, but sometimes it's hard not to tear up a little. It would have been nice to talk about something other than Malcolm with Trump, but I understand why he's so interested in the story since dethroning him is one of my life's great achievements. I've made a mental note for next time to tell him about my bus and how I got a pretty lady to say 'bloody hell' on TV once.

December 2nd 2018

Buenos Aires is so boring. Why couldn't they have had the G20 somewhere fun, like Bali or Fiji? Today I met the grand ruler of Germany, Angela Merkin, who, I'm disappointed to say, didn't even do me the courtesy of learning who I was before our meeting. I understand that Germany is a separatist nation and doesn't engage with the outside world, but I still found it rude. She had a printout of my Wickedpedia page and kept reading it during our conversation. To make matters worse, she'd printed it in English, and since she speaks German as her first language, she kept interrupting me every time she came across a phrase she didn't understand, asking questions like, 'What is a Scomo?' and 'How does one fail upwards?'

December 4th 2018

Let it never be said that I am not a forward-thinking leader. A lot of the gutter journalists at places like the ABC have called me a regressive, but would a regressive leader make the biggest change the Liberal Party has seen in seventy years? Today I made changes to the rules under which a leader can be replaced. From now on the only way I can face a spill is if two-thirds of the party room agrees to it, and as that is unlikely to happen, even with joke votes from my mates intended to stir me up, I will be Prime Minister until I get bored of it and quit.

I am nothing if not polite. And as a polite man, when I walk through a door I like to shut it behind me. It's not my fault if the door has been hanging open for years or is even propped open – I will close it and lock it. It keeps the weather out and prevents any undesirables from following you inside. If I discover a loophole it's the same thing. First, I'll exploit it to make sure it really is a loophole, then once I've seen the benefit it can provide is a real one, I'll close it to make sure it can't be exploited further.

To use another analogy, imagine you're in a pergola in a park and it begins to rain. If the pergola has no doors, pretty soon you will be inundated with people, some potentially homeless, all trying to stay dry. Now imagine if, instead, the pergola has giant lockable gates. Simply by closing them you can sit back, ignore the hundreds of soaking-wet nuisances asking for you to let them in and enjoy the space that is yours by right because you found it first.

December 6th 2018

Parliament has finally adjourned for the year. We really need to do something about this because 65 days of work a year is just too much to ask of people. Thankfully we're not back until the middle of February, so I can enjoy a nice long break, and now that my vacation ban has been lifted I'm finally able to go on a holiday. It's only to Shoalhaven Heads, which isn't overly exciting but it's still a beach, and if I play my cards right I think I can convince Jenny and the girls to go somewhere overseas next year. I've told Jenny the trip will be for her birthday in early January, which is an absolute masterstroke. Firstly, my holiday will serve as her present, eliminating the need to pick something out for her again so soon after Christmas, and secondly, she can't say no, because it's rude to refuse gifts. I can't wait to feel the sand beneath my feet and crack beer after beer after beer. It's been almost three and a half months since I became Prime Minister, I've earned a holiday.

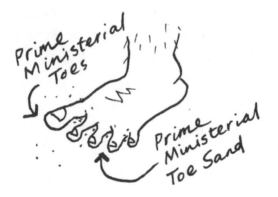

December 9th 2018

Everyone is talking about how I've now lost three Newspolls in a row by 10 points. I'm not sure why. It's a widely known fact that the polls aren't accurate and don't matter. They haven't been a fair representation of public sentiment since they were proof that we needed to remove Malcolm Turnbull from office.

December 13th 2018

With everything starting to quiet down, we decided now would be the perfect time to release Philip Ruddock's Religious Freedom Review, to get it out of the way. Philip has been rattling his crypt door for months now, begging us to 'unleash his masterpiece upon the sinners'. We had to take out some of the more draconian stuff, like publicly stoning unwed mothers and using Chinese weather machines to obliterate rainbows, but the majority of the recommendations were pretty much just common sense.

I mean, if a woman wants an abortion, for example, why shouldn't a doctor be allowed to make her listen to the heartbeat of the foetus on loop for seven days? If women want safe and easy abortions, all they have to do under the recommendations of the report is find a 2000-year-old book that validates their position, which I think is very fair and even-handed.

December 20th 2018

Quick trip to Iraq to meet the troops today. The guys I met are over there fighting ISIS or ISIL or the Taliban or something – it's hard to keep up with which is which. I didn't want to go initially, but my staff convinced me by promising to let me shoot a machine gun. When I arrived they said they didn't feel comfortable letting me use live ammunition, so I just had to do the noise with my mouth, which, if I'm completely honest, wasn't as good.

December 24th 2018

Bill and I have both released our Christmas messages and, although it goes without saying, I absolutely annihilated him. His video just sucks. Firstly, he included his wife in his, which is a big mistake because the fact that such a glamourous woman is married to a man who looks like a magnified Oompa Loompa does nothing but baffle the audience. His video also feels very scripted and it's filmed in an ugly, sterile food bank. Nothing about a giant warehouse used to hand out food to the poor says Christmas to me.

My video, on the other hand, features just me, standing in front of a Christmas tree and some expensive-looking mahogany cabinets, doing what I do best – reading from a teleprompter. I think I hit a real home run with the farmers by saying that the only present I want is rain, but I hope Jenny and the girls don't see the video and take it literally. If all I get for Christmas is some water, I'll be incensed.

There are a few stumbles in the video, including a bit at the end where I tell people to 'stay stafe', but I left them in because they make me seem down to earth. It was also all filmed in one shot, meaning we couldn't cut between multiple angles, so I would have had to do the whole thing over again to fix it, and I really couldn't be stuffed. Anyway, the whole purpose of it was to be better than Bill's and, short of setting the tree on fire and using it to burn an Australian flag, it was always going to be good enough.

December 25th 2018

Merry Christmas!!! My favourite day of the year. As a deeply spiritual man, Christmas is a very special time of year for me. It celebrates the birth of Jesus, but nearly as important, it means I get a lot of presents and can eat three servings of dessert without being scolded by Jenny and the girls. I started the day by opening my gifts. Once again, I got the complete DVD box set of my favourite television program, *Mad Men*. I get this every year, as I play them so much that by the time Christmas rolls around again the discs have been ground down to dust. I also got a framed picture of me with my bus for the study, which, funnily enough, is exactly what I got Jenny. I laughed when I realised we'd gotten each other the same gift, and she smiled so hard it brought tears to her eyes.

After Jenny and the girls made me breakfast, I retired to the lounge room with a beer to watch my DVDs while they got lunch ready. They really outdid themselves with the spread this year – and so did I, managing to put away half a ham, seven roast potatoes, both turkey legs, a few schools of prawns and almost an entire pavlova, all by myself. After all that food I needed a nap and I was thrilled to find, when I woke up at 9 o'clock that evening, that the dishes had all been done and put away. I took the leftover ham and turkey out of the fridge, put on an episode of *Mad Men* and raised my seventeenth beer of the day to another great Christmas.

January 3rd 2019

My first holiday as Prime Minister has finally started! This morning we strapped the canoes to the roof of the car, loaded up the trailer with our bicycles, took a picture for Facebook, then jumped in a comcar bound for Shoalhaven Heads while my staffers put everything back in the garage.

The first thing I did when we arrived was make a beeline for the pub to spend a bit of time among my people. I've been to this hotel before and at any other time of year it would be filled with locals – unseemly types with missing teeth and smelling of fish – but a magical thing happens around Christmas and New Year's. Almost all of Sydney's

"... another great Christmas."

advertising industry moves from the city to the South Coast for their summer break, meaning every pub and restaurant in the area is brimming with people who will practically line up just to shake my hand. The best part is that since they're on holidays they all dress down, making the photos I can get when I walk into the front bar look like I'm being mobbed by the common man, which is great for connecting with voters in areas I don't want to visit. The secret to passing the pub test is finding a pub that is full of people who like you.

There must be a cold going around the offices of Sydney advertising agencies at the moment, because everyone in the bar was sniffling like mad, so I only stayed for eight or nine schooners before heading back to our hotel to spend a bit of time with Jenny and the girls and play on my phone before we went back to the pub for dinner.

It was too difficult to choose between the parmy and the steak, so I ended up getting both, which I think is justified, given I work at least twice as hard as a normal man. As I was leaving, one of the locals spotted me and brought up some issues with me. I've forgotten what they were, but I told him I'd look into what he'd said. He seemed happy and, at the end of the day, isn't making people happy what being Prime Minister is all about?

January 4th 2019

I love fish and chips. I wish I could eat it every day. I wonder if they'd let me put a beach and a fish and chip shop in at Parliament House.

January 9th 2019

Tweeter is a cesspit. It feels like everything I do is pored over and made into 'meems' within minutes. Take the last couple of days, for example. I needed a new photo for my website, so I gathered Jenny and the girls, hired a top-of-the-line photographer and headed to one of Canberra's exclusive private gardens to get some nice product shots of the family. I wore my best beige chinos and a spiffy checked shirt that my image consultant got me from Lowes, and I had Jenny and the girls dress up as the main characters from the movie *Picnic at Hanging Rock*. I am still yet to see the film, but from what I can tell it's about a group of girls who go for a picnic and have a lovely time. A little boring perhaps, not my idea of a good movie – what with the lack of guns and explosions – but definitely in line with the image we were wanting to convey.

The shoot went well and, with the aid of some valium, we even got the dog to calm down long enough to get a few pictures with him that could be used to sell the story that not all animals are afraid of me. All the photographer had to do was touch up the photos, bulk up my muscles a little and maybe add in a smile or two, and we'd have the makings of a fantastic print campaign.

Imagine my horror, then, when I got the final pictures back and realised he hadn't cropped out my shoes! When I'm not in my dress shoes for work, I like to wear sneakers and keep a pair in my office, along with some cargo shorts, chinos and a selection of shirts, for when I forget that it's casual Friday. The photoshoot had been scheduled to take place during my lunch break, so I had planned to change into an outfit from this office wardrobe. When I opened the cupboard, though, I was shocked to find someone had befouled my shoes. Finally, the faint smell that had been hanging around my office since I defeated Dutton in the spill had a source. The photographer was charging by the hour, meaning I didn't have time to go out and buy a new pair, so instead I had to rinse them off in the tearoom sink. There was still quite a bit of staining, but I assumed they would be framed out anyway. Well, they weren't, and now I was left with a selection of photographs in which the horrors visited upon my sneakers were plain for the world to see.

I'd already paid the photographer and, along with the security detail for my recent holiday, my expenses were dangerously close to an amount where people might start to ask questions, so any fix would have to be done in-house. Our intern, Jacob, is quite good at computers, so I asked if he could help me photo-chop some new shoes into the picture. He said he didn't know how to use photo-chop, but he could use a program called Paint, which is essentially the same thing. We went on Google and found a picture of some clean, white shoes; then, as if by magic, I watched as he used it to hide what had been done to my sneakers. Looking at the finished product, I could hardly tell that any digital trickery had even been used.

The trolls on Tweeter must have some sort of program to detect alterations made to photographs, though, as almost immediately they pointed out the change and began to tease me. Before the day was over, photos of me wearing clown shoes began to do the rounds on news sites. I had to get in front of this. Having been a regular guest on 2GB over the years, I've been able to study some of the country's most successful bullies up close, so I knew the most effective tool a bully can employ is embarrassment. The second the victim feels even the smallest amount of shame, they lose. Pride, on the other hand, can defuse a cruel joke immediately. Every ad man knows that with enough self-confidence you can get people to believe anything, even if you don't believe it yourself. Do you think anyone would buy kombucha if its producers admitted that it tastes like a bottle of watered-down vinegar fished out of a drain?

I had my team replace the doctored image with the original, put on my soiled sneakers, Tweetered out a photo with a caption blaming Jacob and promptly had him fired. I was told that by losing his internship at my office he also lost his university scholarship and had to move back to the country, but sometimes sacrifices have to be made for the greater good, and I thanked him with a $20 Target gift card. Hopefully they have Targets where his parents live. It is a shame that this young man had to lose his chance at an education to save me from embarrassment, but this is the kind of harm the Tweeter elite do when they decide to mock me.

January 13th 2019

Just announced a great piece of policy. From 2020, local councils will be forced to have their citizenship ceremonies on Australia Day. If they refuse, they'll be stripped of their right to host a ceremony until they comply. How can we expect new Australians to assimilate if our councils aren't teaching them Australian values like freedom of expression, mateship and a fair go? Only by taking away these freedoms until they submit to the government can we ensure they are appreciated.

January 15th 2019

Guess who's in Vanuatu! I snuck in a 'ministerial visit' to make up for only getting to go to the South Coast, and after a couple of days here I'm heading to Fiji! I've framed it as an economic climate change something or other, but honestly, it's another holiday, which I've been sorely needing since the whole Shoegate business.

The best thing about these ministerial visits is they treat you like a king. You spend a few hours pretending to listen to whoever their leader is, and then it's nothing but feasts and beer and walking on the beach. I brought Jenny along to show her what she'd missed out on for her birthday by making us have our first holiday of 2019 in Australia. I think she might be beginning to understand because she's already had three massages and the tension in her jaw is gone when she smiles. I haven't seen her smile like that since before we started dating.

January 17th 2019

I knew it wouldn't last. I've arrived in Fiji, which should be a cause for celebration, but I've just found out that Bill has ripped off my bus idea. He's currently driving all over Queensland in what he calls the 'Bill Bus'. It doesn't even sound good. He's also been banging on about how he will be riding *inside* the bus the whole time, instead of taking a plane between stops, but I hardly see how that's a selling point. It's going to absolutely stink by the end of it, and advertising how poor the Labor Party is by telling everyone its leader can't afford a plane ticket is a terrible look. I've been so upset by this blatant plagiarism that I've hardly been able to relax. I calmed down a little after my fourth piña colada, but I can't wait to start winning Newspolls so I can call the election and destroy him.

January 20th 2019

I'm sick of all my lady ones leaving the party! My Minister for Ladies, Kelly O'Dwyer, has just announced she won't be contesting the next election, leaving the party looking like it's out of touch and run by blokes. I wish the ladies would just listen to me for once and do what they're told. Tony asked if he could take over her portfolio, as he used to have it when he was Prime Minister, but I said I didn't think it was appropriate for him to be minister for human ladies when he was neither.

January 26th 2019

Australia Day! My favourite day of the year after Christmas and my birthday, only edged out because there're no presents, although I have been trying to get Jenny and the girls to give me one. Today saw rallies around the country calling for the date to be changed, which I thought was fantastic. Australia Day is the perfect time to hold a protest march because it's a public holiday and they're not going to make people late to work. Anyone with a real job has the day off and is spending it eating sausages (Jenny told me I had 17) and drinking beer (32).

January 28th 2019

Looks like Uncle Rupert is beginning to fix the Newspolls. I'm just going to start ignoring my personal approval rating because obviously that's being misreported, but the party's rating is back up to where it was a few months ago when the polls were more accurate. I'm back on track to being able to call an election before I'm forced to in May – calling it that late would be a major embarrassment. What kind of person is so weak they wait until the absolute last minute to act? If I held the election in May, I would be rightfully mocked for being a spineless coward, unable to lead and so frightened of Bill Shorten that I had to be pushed into facing him.

January 30th 2019

I'm up in Queensland again, doing a bit of campaigning with Dutton. It is essential that the public think I like him so

I can use him as a valuable scalp if needed. I had to clarify some statements to a journalist who thought that me saying half of all Australians have never experienced a recession and then following it up with, 'I don't want them to learn how important a strong economy is to each and every single one of them by having them endure the cruel lessons of a weaker economy that would occur under the Labor Party,' meant that I was implying that Labor would plunge the country into a recession if elected. They definitely will, make no mistake, but me putting those two things together is not the same as me saying it outright. I am not a petty man, and I would never stoop to such levels of negative campaigning. Not like Labor. All Labor does is run smear campaigns and ruin economies. The last time we had a Labor government we had a global financial crisis and Kevin Rudd gave the surplus away as cash prizes to the public. He says it was to stimulate the economy and the main reason Australia

avoided a recession, but I walked past his office right after the stimulus payments went out and saw him playing a shiny new Nintendo. It's not hard to see why he was so keen on everyone in the country getting $900.

I told the journalist that all I was saying was that the economy would be weaker under Labor, and if he took that to mean they would drive us into a recession just because of what I'd said immediately before this then that was on him. It's not my fault if people choose to use context to misinterpret the things I say.

February 10th 2019

Another Newspoll and the numbers are exactly the same. I think maybe May 18th would be a good date for the election. Nothing conveys strength like making your opponent wait. I can play the angle that I'm so busy running the country that I don't have time to smash Bill until it's absolutely necessary. I'd like to point out that I'm not being forced into this decision. May 18th is the date I've chosen because it works best for me.

February 12th 2019

Thanks to Malcolm being a sook and Julia Banks being a duplicitous snake, we just lost the right to keep refugees out of the country. Legislation was passed that says asylum seekers detained on Manus Island or Nauru can be forcibly transferred to Australia in the case of a medical emergency. It essentially says to people smugglers that Australia is back open for business. Now all a refugee has to do to set foot on Australian soil is gather up whatever belongings they can carry, spend a bunch of money to get to Asia, spend a bunch more money to secure a spot on a leaky fishing boat, float around in the ocean for a week or two until the Navy picks them up and incarcerates them, become sick enough in one of our detention centres to warrant a medical emergency, then have two doctors agree that they need hospitalisation in Australia. After that, all that needs to happen is for the Minister for Immigration not to overrule the decision because of them having an extensive criminal record, being a terrorist or him just not agreeing with the doctors, as well as the Independent Health Advice Panel not siding with him if he doesn't think they're sick enough – and they're lying in an Australian hospital bed.

The lefties have been trying to argue that this is a very roundabout way of sneaking into the country, especially since being admitted to a local hospital doesn't grant them asylum here, but don't forget that refugees are some of the most desperate people on earth. They'll do almost anything to escape death, poverty and torture, so the metaphorical fences we build to keep them out have to be very tall and pointy.

February 14ᵗʰ 2019

I love Valentine's Day. I got a big box of chocolates from Jenny and the girls to take in and share with my staffers, but I accidentally finished it in the comcar on my way into the office. Luckily, when I got there, I found another box waiting for me. It was from Christopher Pyne, and as soon as we'd used a sniffer dog to find the ones with poison in them, I was free to eat the rest.

I'm beginning to see the bright side to the medevac legislation, too. From this point forward we can start blaming Shorten for every boat of refugees that arrives. As Philip Ruddock regularly wails to me through his crypt door as I seal him in at dawn, 'Find your Tampa and ready the torpedoes!' When John Howard made denying refugees their human rights an election-winning strategy in 2001, he proved just how effective a 'Treat 'em (refugees) mean, keep 'em (Australians) keen' approach can be. This could be my Howard moment, only instead of, 'We decide who comes into this country and the circumstances in which they come,' I'll probably go with, 'Everything is Bill's fault.'

February 18ᵗʰ 2019

I am so sick of Labor's whingeing. I know they have to complain about something to keep up the illusion that they deserve to exist, but it's just so *irritating*. The latest thing they've been kicking up a stink about is wanting me to hold a royal commission into disability abuse, which is outrageous. If we hold a royal commission into something that serious, there's no way I'll be able to sweep the results under the rug or ignore its suggestions. Their pestering has become so annoying, though, that today I cracked and had to pull one of my 'We'll look into it' cards.

Looking into something is a great way to put an issue on the backburner, but this trick can only be used so many times before some a-hole, most likely from the ABC, edits together thirty clips of you saying the same thing and you look like a robot. Repetition is only useful when you want to subliminally implant an idea into someone's head. Jobs and growth. By using a subtle approach, jobs and growth, you can slowly bring them around to your way of thinking. It has taken me many jobs and growth years, but jobs and growth I have mastered this delicate art and can now influence jobs and growth people without them even realising. Right now you probably have the phrase 'jobs and growth' in your head. This is because I have carefully hidden those words throughout the last few sentences without you realising. This is something that we in the advertising and politics industries do on a daily basis to great success. The one I've been using lately is, 'If you have a go, you'll get a go.' I'm not sure what it means yet, but we should find out how people are interpreting it in the next few months.

Hopefully it encourages anyone without a job to stop being unemployed, but we'll just have to wait and see.

Even now that I've revealed this secret, many people will remain unable to detect this practice, but that is purely due to my unrivalled skill. Marketing, when performed by a master, is almost indistinguishable from magic. Jobs and growth.

February 19ᵗʰ 2019

A lot of people have been going on about how much I love coal, which, while true, is said in a way that suggests I'm not supportive of other fossil fuel industries. I'm all for something like natural gas, for example, I'm just less vocal

about it because I got sick of people writing 'Scott loves farts' on the walls of Parliament House.

February 21st 2019

Another one gone. With Julie Bishop's announcement today that she won't be recontesting the next election, there are officially no ladies left in the Liberal Party whose names I remember. We will also have to buy a kettle for the party room now that Julie won't be there to boil water for everyone by staring at it. I know I utterly crushed her during the spill and sent her packing to the backbench, but I never expected her to follow Malcolm out the door – mainly because if anyone was willing to follow him, he wouldn't have needed to be removed as leader. This leaves me in a bit of a bind, politically, as without any lady ones I can name off the top of my head, I'll have to fall back to talking about 'merit' when asked if the party has a problem with women. With people like Craig Kelly in our ranks, this argument is pretty easily disproven.

The problem is that most MPs get their start by being recommended by a friend, and blokes and ladies just don't have that much to talk about. If I have a barbecue at my house, the men all huddle around the grill and watch me turn the sausages until they're pitch black. The ladies might pop over every now and then, but their lungs aren't accustomed to breathing the smoke from the burning meat, so they usually don't stick around long. When it comes time to pick someone for preselection in a safe seat, I can only go with who's in front of me. If I've spent a lot of time in front of the sausages with a chap from down the road, I know, for example, that he owns a business, follows the Sharkies and has never said the N-word, in its entirety, in front of me. His wife might be more qualified, but I've only exchanged brief pleasantries with her, so for all I know she could be a prominent member of a fascist hate group or, even worse, be racist against white people.

At the end of the day I have to choose the man, because although his wife may be better at the job, she is just too much of an unknown. People might wonder why I couldn't just ask Jenny and the girls if the wife is a white supremacist, but they don't have my political eye and besides, I've found that when we get the time to chat, Jenny much prefers to talk about me rather than anything that has happened to her that day.

February 22ⁿᵈ 2019

Dropped by New Zealand this morning to see their Prime Minister, Jacinda Ardern. God, I hate her. She takes up all the global headlines for the region, which is why a lot of people from other countries don't know my name. I mean,

I could bumble around giving people cuddles and paying for their groceries if the only thing I had to do as leader was make sure the gate to the national sheep paddock is locked every night, but I'm in charge of a major nation!

My team says she's so popular because of her use of 'empathy', which I studied back when I was in the advertising industry. Empathy is a social manipulation tactic that can be used to sell a product by convincing the consumer you understand and care about their feelings. It involves things like not looking over someone's shoulder when they're talking to you, listening to what they say and interjecting every now and then with 'I know' or 'That's so sad'. I haven't had to use empathy for a while now, because studies have shown it's largely unimportant to the Liberal voter base, but my team have suggested getting some coaching to brush up on my skills – it's very important to swing voters and will help get my name in the papers overseas. A key indicator of success as an Australian public figure is international recognition, be that for actors, musicians or even politicians. If you're only famous in Australia, you're not really famous – you're practically nobody. I'll have my staff call around and find someone who can provide a bit of empathy training to get me on the front page of the *New York Times*, where I belong.

Normally this trip is meant to be for a weekend, but New Zealand holds no appeal for me, so I cut it down to a single day. The country just lacks the natural beauty of places I normally like to visit, with no beaches, no palm trees and no gentle island breeze. I'm glad it didn't become another island 'state' like Tasmania. I have enough of a problem as it is with how we pretend Tasmanians are Australians without adding two more premiers to begrudgingly shake hands with at COAG.

Jacinda, as lady leaders are wont to do, predictably spent most of our meeting complaining. Her biggest issue seems to be with us deporting New Zealand citizens if they commit a serious crime. She said that it's not fair if one of their people moves to Australia as an infant, is raised there and has no connection to their country of birth, then gets deported if they commit a serious crime. She thinks if they're raised in Australia to become criminals then they should be Australia's problem, but I countered with, 'If

THINGS TO ASK
JACINDA:

1. HOW DO YOU GET PEOPLE TO LET YOU HUG THEM?
2. WHAT SHAMPOO DO YOU USE?
3. STOP TALKING LIKE THAT. (More a request)

they're our problem, why are we allowed to send them to New Zealand?', which must have convinced her because she called my argument 'breathtaking'.

I still don't think she fully appreciates how much being 'tough on crime' resonates with our voter base, though. I told her that Peter had been working on legislation to shoot criminals into the sun with a giant cannon, but until the technology was advanced enough to get them that far we would have to continue to aim it at Auckland. She called me a 'shufty pruck wuth a shut-eatung grun', which I assume is New Zealander for 'strong negotiator', and we left it there.

February 24th 2019

I saw an article in the paper about an old man who had accidentally eaten a tub of paint, thinking it was yoghurt. For a good couple of hours I considered sending a bunch of flowers to Bob Katter in the hospital before I remembered Bob doesn't eat yoghurt or, indeed, any food sold in inner-city supermarkets. As Bob has said to me on a number of occasions, 'If grass, sticks and dead animals I find on the side of the road are so bad for me, then how have I reached 173 years of age?' It's hard to argue with him.

My mistake is not to say I think Bob is so stupid he would accidentally eat paint – I am not saying that at all. Nor am I saying that his brain has been boiled inside his skull by the tropical climate, effectively giving him a form of non-communicable rabies. All I'm saying is that he is from Northern Queensland, and if anyone in Australia was going to consume paint, deliberately or not, I'd expect them to live in the electorate of Kennedy.

February 27th 2019

Bill's still been asking about that bloody royal commission into disability abuse, so I've had to reach a bit further into my bag of tricks to get him off my back. One thing I like to do when everything gets a bit busy is to shift a little of the pressure onto the states. I wrote a letter to all the premiers, asking for them to share the costs of the investigation because it would be too much for the Commonwealth to handle on its own. This should put the final nail in the coffin of this irritating line of questioning from Labor, because the only thing the states hate more than spending money is working together.

Just looking at the East Coast, Victoria thinks there's a rivalry between them and New South Wales; New South Wales thinks there's a rivalry between them and Queensland; and Queensland thinks they're being judged by the rest of Australia for enjoying incest and mid-strength beer. As for the rest of them, South Australia looks down on every other state as convicts; the Northern Territory are baffled by anyone who finishes a sentence in under forty seconds; and Western Australia thinks anyone who doesn't spend half their time living in Bali is too poor to be considered people. We usually forget to send an invite to Tasmania or the ACT because they don't really count. Once I've got enough negative replies, I'll take them back to parliament and really rub Bill's nose in them.

February 28th 2019

Today I announced $50 million worth of grants for businesses to launch programs that help them become more energy efficient. The best thing about announcing a grant scheme is that you can put a massive number on it so it looks like you're spending heaps of money, but then people have to apply for them and those applications can be knocked back. Most businesses won't even get that far, because your average business owner can't be bothered filling out forms. Overall, though, the real key to a good climate policy is making sure it doesn't hurt the economy, so protecting the coal industry is vital. Without coal, there's no point to keeping the climate down because what use is the planet if you've got no money to spend while living on it. The best climate policy, as with any good policy, looks great on paper without actually doing anything.

March 2nd 2019

Christopher Pyne has just announced he'll be retiring from politics and won't be contesting the next election. I'm just relieved it's not another lady one. I'm not sure if it means the entity will be leaving the nineteenth-century wooden doll it inhabits and returning to Hell, or if Christopher will continue to inhabit the doll in the private sector – either way, I'll miss the little scamp. I know it's out of character for a Christian to befriend an ancient, unknowable evil from beyond time, but when he wasn't trying to slice my Achilles tendon with a kitchen knife from beneath the couch or leaving dead goats in my office, his shrieking cackle always brought a smile to my face. When you're in coalition with a bunch of people from the country it's also nice to have someone with an Adelaide accent to posh the place up a bit, although I'm not sure I can ever forgive him for making me try FruChocs. I heard that Steve Ciobo is also retiring, which would probably be more of a concern if anyone knew who he was.

March 4th 2019

They're saying my front bench is in trouble because I've had so many ministers announce their retirement. What they don't seem to realise is that the only difference between the frontbench and the backbench is whether or not I feel like giving you a promotion. I can always restock my cabinet from all of the ones whose names I don't know. Anyway, I've got bigger concerns than learning people's names right now. I've just found out Bill wants to fire all my diplomatic appointments if he gets elected. It's not a big deal because his chances of winning are less than zero, but it's still put me in a mood.

I mean, of course we've appointed a bunch of former Liberal leaders and MPs to these diplomatic posts. They were in the Liberal Party because they were the best of the best. Just because they've left politics doesn't mean they've stopped being great. When I eventually move to the private sector, I will continue to be the most highly qualified leader of whichever company's money I deem worthy to fill my bank account with. Why would we pick someone from the Labor Party when the last election (along with the forthcoming one) showed their members to be nothing but losers? What kind of a Prime Minister would I be if I came out and announced that I'd chosen to appoint the second-best candidates for the jobs just to spare the feelings of the opposition?

Essentially Shorten wants to sack a handful of diplomats because he's jealous of their success. It just goes to show how small and petty a man he really is. Maybe I'll give him a diplomatic appointment after he steps down as leader following his staggering election loss; then, just before he's due to board the plane, I'll fire him. That would show him, the annoying little stain.

March 6th 2019

Labor have just announced their policy for publicly funded abortions, and I could not be more disgusted. I cannot believe they would seek to politicise something that has such wide public support on the eve of an election. Worse still is they had Tanya Plibersek announce it, which is completely unfair. Tanya hasn't had to be leader, so we can't point to a track record of hopelessness and an inability to connect with the public in order to discredit her. If they're going to announce popular policy that we can't adopt, they should at least make Bill hold the press conference so he can butcher the message.

None of that really matters, though, because today all the attention was on me. I rounded up a group of my favourite journalists and flew them to Christmas Island for a press conference and a tour of the facilities. It cost a lot of money, and I've spent over $100 million upgrading it, but asylum seekers need to know that if they get sick, but not sick enough to be transferred to a proper hospital on the mainland, they could end up here, which adds another step to their nefarious 'get to Asia, get on a boat, get locked up, get very sick, get to Australia then somehow stay' plan.

After we had a walk around and the photographers took some good shots of me with the razor wire, we jumped back on the plane and flew the 5000 kilometres back. Some might say that over thirteen hours of travel time in one day is too much for a press conference, but if we'd made people spend the night on Christmas Island, no one would have come. The accommodation there is dreadful.

March 8th 2019

The Tweeterverse is out to get me again. All I said was that if ladies wanted better treatment in the workplace, that shouldn't mean men are treated worse. They think that it's offensive that I said this on International Women's Day, but I honestly don't see anything wrong with it. Equality should be about lifting everybody up, not making compromises and bringing one side down to make that more achievable. I'm all for more female CEOs but not at the expense of all the male CEOs who currently hold those positions. If a lady wants to be the boss, she should start her own company or find a job vacancy that no men who are equally qualified or better connected have also applied for. If there's only so much money to go around in a certain organisation and paying women equally means the men earn less, I just don't think that's fair. Those men have gotten used to earning that much. If all of a sudden they're making twenty per cent less, what will that do to their weekly budgets? How are they meant to survive?

If the ladies in the company, on the other hand, have been making do with a lower salary for the entirety of their careers and they're doing just fine, then what is the point in paying them more? All you're doing is finding a problem where there isn't one and solving it by hurting the men and giving the ladies an amount of money that will only serve to confuse them. If the company finds some more money in the budget for wages, then sure, pay the women more, but the men should also get a raise because that's equality. In the end, isn't that what International Women's Day is all about?

March 9th 2019

My Women's Day speech made it onto CNN! They said I'd 'caused outrage' but I was the only one mentioned by name, so that's great news for me. The more people talking about me the better. I am a firm believer in the theory that any publicity is good publicity. Just look at that Laura Bimble girl who I put in my famous Tourism Australia ad. No one knew who she was before I made her say a swearword on telly, and now she's married to a Hemsworth or something.

March 10th 2019

Newspoll can go stuff itself.

March 11th 2019

Barnaby Joyce and my deputy have been fighting again.
Barnaby upset, I think Colin is his name, by saying that if
there was a spill he would stand because he was voted in
at the last election, so he deserves to be the leader. I can
understand why this annoyed Colin – or maybe Eugene –
because everyone knows that the only leader people vote
for is the leader of the Liberal Party, because he (or she, but
that's extremely unlikely) is the one who gets to be Prime
Minister. Colin or Eugene or Nigel fired back by comparing
the Coalition to a successful marriage that, given Barnaby's
old family has been publicly burning an effigy of him every
Sunday morning before church, some saw as a bit of a low
blow. Hopefully everything sorts itself out soon, though, as
the Nationals are an integral part of our hold on power. In
a lot of country seats the voters refuse to elect anyone with
more than eighty per cent human DNA. The question could
be raised as to why we don't just recruit our own subhuman
candidates to run in those electorates, but that would mean
allowing them into the party room and, as anyone who has
spent time with Matt Canavan or George Christensen can
tell you, extended contact with people from the country can

lead to a feeling similar to seasickness that can last for days. It's much better for everyone if they have their own party room, in this case a lead-lined box two kilometres beneath Parliament House, and we only have to see them in the chamber or in one-on-one meetings where their effects can be neutralised with various talismans and carbon rods.

March 14th 2019

I'm thinking of passing a law that makes it illegal to protest. Thousands of children from all over the country are planning to leave school to protest the climate by blocking traffic and chanting the same little rhymes hippies have been shouting for years as if they mean something. There was a time when I wouldn't have been concerned with the kids of lefties wagging school, with truancy leading to failing, which would prevent them from becoming politicians through university connections, but as Pauline Hanson has proven, people don't even have to graduate kindergarten to get into parliament these days. It's not really the fault of the children, though – it's the schools I blame. If there was a mandatory History of Coal class or economics was taught at primary school I'm sure they'd be singing a different tune. Their signs may be calling me a 'massive wankstain' now, but they'll be thanking me in fifteen years when they've all got enough money to afford air conditioners to deal with how hot our summers are predicted to get.

March 15th 2019

I really want to get along with Pauline Hanson. She sends a good number of votes our way, but God she makes it hard sometimes. If it wasn't for the fact that her single qualification for One Nation candidates is 'breathing', I wouldn't be in a position where I have to publicly agree with Labor and the Greens. Much like the sky being blue, it's a pretty basic thing to agree on the universal truth that Fraser Anning is a terrible person, but we're about to head into an election campaign and I need as much distance between me and Bill as I can get.

Fraser ended up in the senate after another One Nation senator, Malcolm Roberts, was deemed ineligible to stand for a far-right party due to his foreign citizenship. Once he was disqualified, Anning's 19 first preference votes were apparently enough to get him over the line. Within an hour of being sworn in he had left One Nation and then made headlines by evoking Hitler in his maiden speech by calling for a 'final solution' for immigration and championing the return of the White Australia policy.

The thing that always confuses me about white supremacists is that, for all their talk of being the master race, the loudest supporters of their cause aren't exactly what most people would consider 'genetically superior'. I could maybe understand Anning wanting a country full of people like him if he had the looks of someone like Chris Hemsworth or was incredibly bright or successful, but he's none of those things. He owes hundreds of thousands of dollars to creditors of his failed business, and looks like if someone's least favourite uncle had a baby with an old shoe and it grew up to be the manager of an unsuccessful suburban swimming pool. I wouldn't expect a nation of Fraser Annings to be capable of mastering fire, much less the rest of the world.

One thing he has mastered, though, is getting his name in the paper by being awful. New Zealand is suffering through a horrific tragedy in which a large number of Muslim people were murdered, and Anning, in an admittedly very successful cry for attention, Tweetered out that it was because of Islamic immigration. Race-baiting is something that every politician does – Australia is a country that responds very well to a bit of 'fear of the other' – but what

Anning has done today has just ruined it for the rest of us. Now whenever we want to subtly refer to people 'not adapting to our way of life' or suggest that refugees could be sex criminals, it will conjure up the image of a decaying goblin from Queensland using the bodies of forty-nine murder victims as political capital. It will take months before Australia forgets that preference deals with the far-right lead to the election of people like Fraser, and the election is meant to happen before the end of May!

I'm going to have to come up with a new campaign approach for Queensland . . .

March 16th 2019

Some kid smashed an egg on the back of Anning's head at a Nazi rally today, and I've already watched the video about thirty times. As a government we cannot condone any act of violence upon a politician, whether they were democratically elected or slithered up through the s-bend of the toilet with 19 first preference votes, so everyone at Parliament House is having to enjoy this in private. It's the most unified I've seen Australian politics in my twelve years in parliament. Even Cory Bernardi, who is meant to be Fraser's friend, said he laughed while watching it, and I haven't seen a genuine smile out of Cory since I walked in on him lashing himself with a cat-o'-nine-tails for what he told me was the grave sin of accidentally thinking the word 'boobies'.

It's a shame we're not allowed to publicly celebrate the boy, because he's the first person I've thought deserving of a knighthood since Tony Abbott tried to demote Prince Philip by making him a Knight of the Order of Australia. I might not agree with the rest of his politics, but it would be pretty hard to argue that the far right don't deserve to have eggs cracked over them. It's why we sent so many of our troops into the trenches in World War II. Unfortunately, their preferences flow towards us, so during the upcoming election campaign we'll have to make sure these pranks don't escalate and scare them away. When not emboldened they're quite timid creatures, and the threat of an egg or some flour or, indeed, any cake ingredient, over the head might have a great deal of them abandoning the voting queue and staying home with their parents. I think I speak for all Australians, though, when I say that once the election has been won, I hope they are showered in as many eggs as the chickens of this great country can lay.

March 19th 2019
Another Morrison Masterstroke™ today. I've just announced my plan for stopping migrants from clogging up our roads. Along with bringing the yearly migration

cap down by thirty thousand, I'm also going to make them live in the bush for three years before they can apply for permanent residency. In my travels to the darkest corners of Australia, the one thing I've noticed about its rural electorates, aside from the smell, is how little traffic there is. There are so few vehicles on the road that everyone can, and does, drive at least forty over the speed limit. Anything less and they'll throw empty rum bottles at your car and try to run you off the road. Traffic has never been a huge issue for me, as I've been allowed to turn up and leave at whatever time I choose in every job I've had, but polling has told us that being stuck in a gridlock is one of the biggest daily annoyances for middle-class Australians, so announcing a policy that targets this, even if it only keeps the problem at its current level, is a major vote-winner.

Out in the bush there's plenty of room for everyone, even if we tripled the numbers, plus these immigrants are highly unlikely to last the three years required to move to the city if their only available pastimes are shopping at Target Country and being racially abused. One thing we've realised after many successful years in government is that all your average Australian really wants is to be better off than his neighbour, which means either making his life better or making his neighbour's life worse. Both options have the same outcome but the second one is a lot cheaper, so the decision is a no-brainer, and given that permanent residents can't vote, we won't be pissing off anyone who actually matters or endangering any National seats by adding people capable of rational thought to their electorates.

March 21st 2019

Those sneaky turds at *The Project* tried to ambush me today, but I was way too clever for them. I thought they wanted me to drop in for a chat and throw to some funny videos that a junior researcher had found on YouTube, like they've had Rove's friend doing since Dave Hughes became too successful for the job. Imagine my surprise, then, when I turn up to find Waleed bloody Aly wanting to do a one-on-one interview with me about Muslims. I've never understood the appeal of Waleed. People on the left act like he's this great journalist, but he speaks so softly that you can easily just shout over the top of him to win every interview.

There's been a bit of talk about Muslims in the news lately after the tragedy in New Zealand, and it's amplified an old story about me saying in a shadow cabinet meeting in 2010 that we should use anti-Islamic sentiment in the community to chase votes. That's too long ago to remember if it even happened or not, but I want to make perfectly clear that if any kind of bigotry leads to the murder of innocent men, women and children, that is too much bigotry and things have gone too far. I condemn, absolutely, any

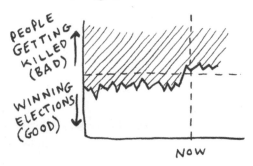

BIGOTRY LEVELS

PEOPLE GETTING KILLED (BAD)

WINNING ELECTIONS (GOOD)

NOW

Islamophobia that leads to a massacre, and that has always been my position on the matter.

Waleed was stuck in the past and wanting to talk about that meeting, though, so I had to approach the interview like any grilling from the press and deploy my full arsenal of argument-winning tactics. First, I sat as far back in my chair as possible, almost lying down, to show how little I cared about my opponent. As all the coolest movie stars have proven, the second you care about anything you're a loser. Waleed predictably sat on the edge of his seat like a nervous little girl at a piano recital. I'd already won before we started, but I decided to press on to teach him a lesson.

Aly began to speak in his usual, simpering, 'I'm clever and everything is serious' tone and I unleashed my second weapon on him. Everything he asked or proposed, I just said the opposite but louder. If we can learn anything from the fantastic work done by the coal industry on climate change over the last few years, it's that denial plus volume equals victory. If you're listening to two people argue, you're most likely to agree with the loudest voice. Volume conveys power and strength, and by flatly denying everything your opponent says, there's no way they can use logic to trap you. The second you concede even the slightest bit of ground, they'll have you contradicting yourself, admitting to things and eventually telling the whole truth rather than just the truth you want people to hear.

I interrupted, spoke over Waleed and grinned my way through over half an hour of questions before, utterly defeated, he conceded with the requisite, 'Thank you for your time.' Victory is always sweet, but it's even sweeter when you're not expecting it. I woke up this morning

thinking the highlight of my day would be pretending to have found a funny animal video on YouTube but ended it with one of the heroes of the Left bending the knee in deference to me, Scott Morrison, master debater. I can't wait to call the election so I can do this every day.

March 23rd 2019

Gladys Berjejrjkijlkkjijln just won the New South Wales election, so it looks like my popularity is rubbing off on a state level. I think there must be something wrong with the phone lines, though, as she hasn't called to thank me yet. Not that I need her to – if she can't get through I still know how appreciative she, and all Liberals at a state level, are. I walked into a meeting with Gladys once and heard her say, 'Oh great, his Royal Highness is here,' under her breath. I know I wasn't meant to hear it, but I do see myself as the King of Australia, so it's good to know that my loyal subjects think of me in the same way.

March 26th 2019

A few articles have been published lately suggesting my support of Malcolm two days before I replaced him is proof that I'm duplicitous or two-faced. For some reason they think when I said, 'This is my leader and I'm ambitious for him,' it meant I would fight tooth and nail to keep him in the job, but at no point does the quote suggest that. He was, at the time, my leader, and I was ambitious for him. The fact that that ambition was for his career in the private sector rather than as Prime Minister doesn't make what I said a lie. Once again, the media has used the context in which things were said to prescribe meaning to a deliberately ambiguous statement.

TWO DAYS BEFORE

If I'd supported him moving forward as Prime Minister, I would have said that, and even if I did mean that at the time, like all great ad men I left things vague enough that my intention could be changed in retrospect. This is a key lesson for anyone in the public eye. As long as you keep everything you say slightly unclear you can wait to see what the general consensus is before you ascribe it a value. By leaving the option on the table to say, 'Yeah, that's what I meant,' you can always be on the right side of history. It's tempting to have convictions from the beginning and stick to them, but don't be drawn into that trap. A true leader knows to only decide what they believe once they know which opinion is the most beneficial to their popularity.

March 27th 2019

Today we were forced to make some tough decisions and place One Nation beneath the Labor Party on our how-to-vote cards. Trust me, I would love nothing more than to put Bill and his gang of union goobers dead last, but members of Pauline's little chapter have been filmed trying to solicit donations from American gun lobbyists and promising to weaken Australia's restrictions on firearms. To top it all off, the Imperial Wizard of One Nation, Pauline herself, was caught on tape appearing to question whether the Port Arthur massacre was a conspiracy set up by the government.

Now, I don't care what anyone's personal beliefs are, as long as they keep them to themselves, but when you start to question the actions and policy of the great John Howard, you've gone too far. We cannot sit idly by as the infallible word of John is defied so brazenly, and so we have taken a stand. This is entirely about taking the moral high ground and doing what's right, but that aside, it's pretty much guaranteed that One Nation will still place us above Labor, and at the end of the day, that's the only part of the preference deal that really matters to us.

April 1st 2019

Today was April Fool's Day and Christopher Pyne got me a beauty, hiding under my desk and sticking me in the leg with a needle full of tranquiliser. When I woke up I was tied to a chair and Christopher was doing his little Rumpelstiltskin dance and splashing me with petrol from a jerry can. He was threatening to cut my ear off and light me on fire when Parliament House security broke down the door and caught him in what they call the 'Pyne net'.

It's this sort of good-natured prank that I'll miss the most about not having Christopher around. Other members of the Liberal Party have pretended to make attempts on my life to wind me up, but no one else seems to have Pyne's sense of theatre or dramatic flair. Not having him in my cabinet might save the money we currently have budgeted to spend on burning sage, but things will certainly be a lot less entertaining.

"Christopher was doing his little
Rumpelstiltskin dance..."

April 2nd 2019

I'm incredibly proud of Josh Frydenberg. He's come
up with a genius way of buying votes at the election.
Normally paying people to vote for you is illegal, but
Josh has worked out a way around this. By disguising
this money as a tax break and rebate, then saying the
legislation won't be passed unless we win, we can
effectively hide the bribe in plain sight. Better yet, we
don't even have to use our own money – it will come from
cuts to the National Disability Insurance Scheme, which,
being a Labor program, was probably incredibly wasteful
anyway.

As if that wasn't enough, though, the budget is also
in surplus, which I've decided to advertise with a quick
print campaign. The ad centres around a picture of
me looking strong and clever, with the slogan 'Back in
Black', which I'm told is a popular rock song. Some have
wrongly suggested that it should be Frydenberg in the
pictures because none of my three budgets as Treasurer
were in surplus, but that doesn't take into account all the
groundwork I put in that made Josh's job as easy as it was,
or how inspired he was by having me as his leader. If I had
handed down a fourth budget, who's to say that wouldn't
have been in surplus too? Unfortunately for my detractors
there's no way of proving otherwise because I'm now
Prime Minister, so I'll never have to do one again.

Other haters are also saying it's foolish to celebrate my surplus in advance because a lot can happen in a year, but really, what's the worst that could happen? I am 100 per cent confident that the next twelve months will be smooth sailing. Some may call the mugs I'm having made up with the 'Back in Black' slogan on them premature, but Josh's budget says I'm delivering a surplus, so why should I have to wait the full year until I've actually delivered it before I receive my duly-earned praise?

April 3rd 2019

A couple of reporters are upset that I've decided to close the facility on Christmas Island in July. They seem to think that just because it will never be used, the $180 million we spent on upgrading it was a waste of money. I disagree. I think that the only reason we didn't see huge numbers of extra asylum seekers making their way to Australia is that they saw my press conference and pictures of me wandering around the island on the internet. Besides, $180 million is a drop in the ocean compared to the $1.4 billion I'd earmarked for it over the next four years. I delivered taxpayers the same result for just a fraction of the cost. Sure, they might ask the question of whether extra refugees were ever really a problem, but I prefer not to deal in hypotheticals. In the real world, I spent just under

$200 million doing up a closed detention centre, flew a plane load of reporters six and a half hours there, walked around for a bit, flew them home again and then abandoned the scheme because it was unnecessary.

Based on that evidence, the only conclusion that can logically be drawn is that the centre was only made unnecessary by me opening it in the first place and that $180 million was a *bargain* compared to how much it would have cost if we'd actually had to use it. For someone like Bill Shorten this would be a crowning achievement, although it would have cost much more because Labor doesn't know how to manage the economy, but for me it is just another feather in my already over-stuffed cap.

April 4th 2019

Bill delivered his budget reply today, but to be honest I wasn't listening. It's very hard to listen when he speaks. When he's finally booted out of parliament I expect business will probably drop off at the Parliament House coffee cart, as staying awake during Question Time will be a lot easier.

April 5th 2019

Today I officially launched my royal commission into abuse of people with disabilities. I came up with the idea a while

ago and I've been working on it ever since. I sent a letter to the states asking for their support, because it was going to take a lot of work and resources, and they all came through. I think it says a lot about how kind and generous I am as a man that it was me who brought this to fruition and not Bill Shorten or, indeed, anyone from the Labor Party.

When I was making my speech, my team stressed that I had to apply all the empathy I could, so I spent the last few days working on it with my coach. She said that the main thing to focus on was imagining what it must be like to be abused, so during my speech I tried to picture people insulting me and being cruel, only not as a joke like it normally is. This technique worked brilliantly! As I was speaking, I actually began to cry a little! I must point out, though, this was not me crying. I would never do that because I am not a lady or a member of the Greens – this was the Scott I had imagined in my head, one who people don't think is great and who isn't the world's best Prime Minister. If there were any doubts about just how creative I am, the fact that I was able to conjure up a version of myself who isn't universally loved should definitely put them to rest.

April 6th 2019

Bill is practically begging me to call the election, but I'll do that when I'm good and ready. I've got my deputy's deputy, Bridget McKenzie, doling out sports grants to marginal seats. We're technically not allowed to do that if we're in caretaker mode – and in case Bill hasn't noticed, I'm the Prime Minister – so I'll announce the date when it suits me. I've told Bridget not to involve me too much because, while everything is completely legal and above board, and there's absolutely nothing dodgy going on, I'll need someone to take the fall for this scheme if people ever find out about it. I decided to give this job to the Nationals because farmers are used to getting their hands dirty, even if the majority of them are millionaires who employ other people to work their land.

April 7th 2019

Massive surge in my Newspoll numbers today. Newspoll
is the most accurate way of gauging public sentiment, and
it doesn't take a mathematical genius to see that a jump of
two points, putting me at my highest levels so far, means
people are really digging what I'm laying down. My personal
approval rating is also up at record levels for me, while Bill's
continues to drop, really ramming home just how much of
a loser he is. Time to call the election.

April 8th 2019

A bunch of vegans glued themselves to the road in
Melbourne this morning. I wonder if they know that
superglue is made from horses' hooves. Of course it
happened in Melbourne, though, a city that answers the
question, 'What if Sydney was crap?'

April 11th 2019

No going back now. I've officially called the election for
May 18th, and now we enter a month of what I do best.
I'm so excited to get stuck in and make as many ads as our
donors can afford to fund from their secret bank accounts.
I can't wait to see the first billboard go up, the fifteen-second
spots to roll out during *A Current Affair*, to call Bill a shifty

little gopher with a head like a bollard. I'm going to make my prediction for the result right here. I am going to win ~~150~~ 77 seats for the Coalition. I guarantee it.

April 12th 2019

Things probably haven't gotten off to the best start. Peter Dutton has accused his opponent, who only has one leg, of using her disability as an excuse for why she doesn't live in the electorate. She has said she hasn't been able to find a house that is accessible but that she'll buy one and modify it if she gets elected, to which Peter has said, 'Bulls**t.' Fair enough, too, because Peter still lives there despite the disability of having his soul ripped to pieces and attached to seven hidden treasures, although it must be said he did this himself to achieve a kind of immortality. But a bunch of journalists have picked up on his comments and are now accusing Dutton of being insensitive. While maybe it is true that Dutton is an undead snake-man who cannot feel affection, this also paints me in a negative light, and as a warm-hearted, dinky-di Aussie bloke, brimming with love and kindness, that's just not fair. It would have been far better for our campaign if the press had gone the right way with the story and run a hit piece on the woman with one leg.

April 13th 2019

I shook a lot of hands yesterday on my first day of campaigning, so today I gave myself some well-earned downtime and took Jenny to the races. Horseracing was something that had never really taken my fancy before, but when I found out there were a number of successful Australians I could cheer for, I treated it like swimming during the Olympics and developed a keen, temporary interest.

Racehorses, to me, epitomise this great country and the spirit of the Aussie battler. Claimed at birth by a number of wealthy investors and beaten into submission by their trainers, their fear of a riding crop is unrivalled, given how fast they run when threatened with one. It's not just their fearful scrambling I admire, though: like all good Aussie battlers, they continue to make their owners money long after retirement. If they can manage to make it through their career without breaking a leg and needing to be shot to death in front of the crowd, they can be regularly harvested of seed or impregnated and their children sold for hundreds of thousands of dollars.

What is more Aussie than a worker who goes above and beyond to make their bosses lots of money? It's exactly what I mean when I say, 'If you have a go, you'll get a go.' Sure, these horses could stay home when they're a bit sore, or have weekends off, or simply shatter their shin bones and lie back, waiting to be destroyed, but think of all the cash that would be lost. No, when these magnificent beasts wake up each morning they say to themselves, 'I am going to go out there and panic harder than every other horse. I am going to panic so hard that I beat them all. The only thing that scares me more than the goblin on my back is my owners not making every cent they can.' The most impressive part of all this, though, is that with the blood, sweat and equine tears poured into the industry, no horse has ever felt the need to form a union. They truly are Australian heroes.

After the races I was a bit peckish, so I took Jenny over to Strathfield to get some dim sims. I saw an Asian lady and, the cameras being right there, took my opportunity to do a bit of on-the-fly campaigning and pulled out a perfect, 'Ni hao,' which is Asian for, 'How do you do?' I assume she misheard and thought I'd asked where she was from because she responded with, 'I'm Korean,' but I didn't want to embarrass her by pointing out her mistake, so I simply smiled and moved on. All in all this little trip was a success, though, as I walked away with seventeen deep-fried dim sims for my dinner and a salad for Jenny, which she told me was very nice.

April 14th 2019

You'd think, being a Sunday, I'd be allowed to have today off, but no. Even God gets to take Sunday off, but

apparently I have to attend a campaign rally in Brisbane. At least there will be a lot of people chanting my name and clapping for me, which is kind of similar to what God will be doing, but I am still in desperate need of a holiday.

April 15th 2019

I've just seen that Matt Canavan has posted a Tweeter video of himself eating a raw onion in homage to Tony Abbott. For anyone outside of Queensland this might look like campaign suicide, but it's actually a very clever move. People that far north are deeply suspicious of what they call 'book learnin'', so things like eating raw onions, sticking knives in toasters and chewing stones to clean your teeth are all major vote-winners in those electorates. They actually used to elect MPs via a contest where the man (women were banned) who ate the most rat poison without dying was given the seat. Thankfully this process ended in the late '90s and, with Warren Truss and Bruce Scott's retirement at the last election, there are no longer any Queensland Nationals who earned their way into parliament in this manner. Some still do it, of course. George Christensen, for example, will go through a couple of packets a day, but this is because, according to him, 'Poison make George strong.'

April 16th 2019

It seems Matt eating that onion has summoned Tony Abbott's ghost from beyond the grave that is northern Sydney. Apparently he told reporters that, while he wasn't seeking it, if we lose the election he would be open to accepting the party leadership if it was offered to him. Tony used to be a boxer, so I try not to hold what he says against him given how much has happened to his brain, but to suggest that we might lose the election is unforgivable. Unfortunately, I don't know what options I have left to punish him. He's been on the backbench since Malcolm rolled him, so it's not like I can demote him any further, and he already has to spend the rest of his life being

Tony Abbott, so any penalty I can come up with will seem like nothing in comparison. Maybe I'll just have Jenny and the girls drive over to his house and let the tyres down on his bike.

I spent the day campaigning for one of my few remaining lady ones in the electorate of Corangamite, because if I'm going to be in Victoria I may as well be in the one place where the beaches aren't garbage. The electorate boundaries have recently changed, so she'll probably lose her seat, but hopefully by having me stand next to her at a press conference people will remember that a vote for her is a vote for me, and my massive popularity will carry her over the line. It's no big deal if it doesn't, though – she was a Turnbull supporter.

April 17th 2019

I normally wouldn't visit Tasmania during an election since it's not part of Australia, but they offered me free ice-cream, so I jumped on a plane this morning and headed to Devonport. On the press bus, which I decided to ride to keep tabs on what they were saying about me, someone mentioned that the island was technically a state and that five MPs and six senators come from here, meaning Jacqui Lambie wasn't just in the senate as part of a work-for-the-dole scheme like I'd thought. Realising that, along with the free ice-cream, I could also use this trip to do a bit of campaigning, I quickly bashed together a little $100 million pledge for irrigation and announced it when we stopped off to look at a farm. I'm not entirely sure what irrigation is, but I was pretty sure it had something to do with farmers, and given their smiles after my announcement, I think I was right.

People often mistakenly hold the belief that a leader should understand every piece of legislation they announce, but this is incorrect. All a leader really needs to know is if an announcement is going to make them more or less popular – the reasons why are completely superfluous and only serve to complicate matters. Whenever one of my ministers brings me a proposal, the only question I ask is, 'Will this end up with more people liking me?' If the answer is yes, consider that proposal green-lit.

The tasting spoons at the ice-cream factory were tiny, so it took a long time before I was full, but I got there eventually.

April 18th 2019

Clive Palmer has announced himself as the top senate pick for his 'party'. I assume he's run out of places to have naps in his mansion and misses the comfortable seats of the crossbench.

April 19th 2019

Good Friday. Sure it's a holiday, giving me a much-needed break, but it's the absolute worst day of the Easter period. It's the date that Jesus (the second best member of the Holy Trinity) was crucified, and I've got a whole two days before the Easter Bunny comes to give me my chocolate eggs. To make matters worse, I also ran into Tony Abbott at church. Having a conversation with Abbott is awkward at the best of times, given the propensity for the microchip in his brain to glitch, causing him to silently shake for a few minutes while it reboots, but after his comments on taking over the leadership I could barely look him in his glowing, red eyes.

I saw on the news that Bill Shorten didn't even bother going to church. He was feeding the poor with the Salvation Army. I don't want to presume anything, but I think I speak for Jesus when I say he should have been at his local parish

instead. Today is a day for paying respect to the Son of God and his noble sacrifice, not for winning points by doing charity work. Sit your bum in the pew, sing a little song and fill up the collection plate. That's what being a man of faith is all about. The homeless will still be there tomorrow and you can get all the photo ops you like, but for this one day those photographs need to be taken in church.

April 20th 2019

I found where Jenny was hiding the Easter eggs and decided to give myself a little pre-Easter treat for all my hard work on the campaign so far, but I may have gotten a little carried away because before I knew it I was waking up in a pile of coloured foil. Not to worry though, I've sent Jenny to the shops to pick up some more so that me and the girls won't be disappointed tomorrow morning. I've also asked her to do a better job of hiding them so this doesn't happen again. For us to wake up tomorrow and not have any chocolate to eat would have ruined Easter.

April 21st 2019

I wish Jenny had bought more chocolate eggs. She only got me three big ones and a couple of bags of little ones, so after I'd finished them I had to raid the girls' baskets, which really upset them. After this traditional Easter breakfast, we headed to church again, this time to get some pictures that show off just how connected I really am. I had my photographer capture me speaking directly to God himself and sent the photos straight to the press. It only took the Tweeter haters a few minutes before they started calling my incredibly impressive pictures 'creepy', saying that me lifting my hand up to connect with Jesus looked like a Nazi salute.

As I've already said, I am not a Nazi – the fact that the extreme right's preferences flow to us is just a happy coincidence. It's typical of the Left to mock a man for his beliefs, though. I am just a humble servant of God, and to be ridiculed for trying to share my faith with the world through some carefully planned campaign pictures is beyond the pale. What kind of person sees a great leader giving inspiration to millions of Australians and increasing his popular vote during an election and decides to make a joke of it? This is exactly like what happened with Jesus. From this day forth, Easter Sunday will be the new Good Friday – the day I was unfairly crucified for the simple act of spreading the Good Word and promoting the Liberal Party faith while Barabbas Shorten was allowed to attend his own church without so much as a snicker from the baying Tweeter mob. I was so upset when my staffers told me about this cyber abuse that Jenny had to drive around to three different supermarkets to gather enough discount Easter eggs to calm me down.

April 22nd 2019

There's been some chatter from the Labor side about a water buyback scheme that Barnaby was in charge of a couple of years ago. Aside from this not having anything to do with me, I just can't find it in myself to care. I'm sure what the Nationals do in the country is interesting to them, but the second someone starts talking about silos or basins or how dirt is red in some places, I just drift off. Not being across the issue works to my benefit, though. I'll never look like I'm lying if I genuinely don't know the answer to a question. The Labor Party have always been experts in general stupidity, but they have yet to cotton on to how effective tactical ignorance can be when facing a potential scandal. After all, I can't cover up what I don't care enough about to understand.

April 23rd 2019

The party released an absolute belter of an ad today. It's a smear campaign, which is my favourite type of political advertising – as long as it's not being made by Labor. In the ad we run a clip of Julia Gillard saying she wouldn't introduce a carbon tax, then follow it with Shorten claiming he won't bring in a death tax, the implication being that since one Labor leader changed their mind on a policy, the current one will definitely do the same thing. Bill has come out and called the ad a lie, but here's the genius of it: we never said he was definitely going to go back on his word. All we've done is put a former Prime Minister's words next to his and let the public come to the conclusion that he's a dodgy little creep all on their own.

The commercial finishes with the slogan 'The Bill Australia can't afford' and a picture of him looking like there's something wrong with his brain, which brilliantly conveys our party line that Shorten is a complete bumworm and no one should vote for him. The beautiful part of this kind of campaign is that we can use it to discredit almost everything he says. If, only one short decade ago, Julia Gillard introduced a carbon tax after saying she wasn't going to, then what else is Bill lying about? I've currently got my team working overtime to find some footage of Bill promising not to murder fifty per cent of the population, or something similar, to make the next one.

April 24ᵗʰ 2019

Once again Bill has copied my work. Labor put out an ad today with footage of me telling Neil Mitchell in a radio interview that we wouldn't rule out a death tax. In typical Shorten fashion, though, the imitation pales in comparison to the superior original. While our ad shows Bill taking a clear position on a new tax while implying he's a liar, theirs only shows me lithely dancing around Neil's questions and refusing to take a position one way or the other. You can't call someone a liar if they haven't committed to anything. Fairly soon it will be proven just how out of their depth Labor are when they realise how difficult it is to pin down a man who stands for nothing.

April 25ᵗʰ 2019

Today is Anzac Day, giving me another chance to take some downtime. Anzac Day is not about celebration, though. It is a day to remember the sacrifices of all the young men who died protecting this country and pay respects to them

IDEA

Anzac biscuits in shape of Anzac Cove? Yummy, but also more of a reminder?

by sombrely drinking a lot of beer and gambling at the pub, then solemnly eating tray after tray of delicious, chewy biscuits that Jenny bakes.

April 26th 2019

A rumour has been circulating for some time that I once soiled myself in a McDonald's after a football game. On the surface, many people would think this is an embarrassment unbecoming of a leader, but let me ask you a question: would you still think this way if you found out that this rumour was actually a work of marketing genius? It's a widely known fact that all Australian men will go number two in their pants around once or twice a year. We all do it, no big deal – we just don't talk about it. Imagine for a second, though, that you've just been to a Sharks game, and the pie, sausage roll, three dim sims and 600ml Pepsi Max you had at half-time have gone right through you. The traffic is so heavy that you'll never make it home in time, so you pull into the nearest fast-food restaurant, which just happens to be a McDonald's, to do your business. You make a beeline for the counter to buy a Big Mac and a Frozen Coke, because the rule at McDonald's is that toilets are *for customers only*. Rules are incredibly important. They are what separate us from the animals – without them, a man is no better than a monkey flinging excrement at the walls of its enclosure at the local zoo, or someone from the Western Suburbs. Some people might be happy to just buy something cheap, like an apple pie or something from the snack menu, but I refuse to be so cheap. Besides which, I love Big Macs and getting to use the toilet while eating a delicious hamburger is killing two birds with one stone. If you're not willing to spend at least five dollars, then jog on, I say! My dear friend Alan Jones doesn't eat McDonald's because they are not a major sponsor of his show, which is fair enough, and as such he will only use public toilets. I admire his integrity.

Anyway, back to McDonald's . . . Let's say there's a big line, so you have to wait. Fifteen minutes later, your order is finally ready and you're absolutely busting. You're halfway to the men's and have just taken your first bite of hamburger when you feel something warm running down your leg. In all your effort to clench your backside, you've inadvertently completely relaxed your front side. You try to shuffle faster, to get to the toilet, but this causes you to unclench your buttocks, and now you're dealing with what some people call a 'number three'.

Now, I'm not saying this happened to me, but if it did, this is how I would handle it. Every situation, even one as embarrassing as this, is just a marketing opportunity in disguise, so I would start by reframing the narrative. By allowing the rumour to spread that I'd shat myself at

Engadine Maccas, I could successfully head off the real story that I shat *and* wet myself. No one hearing the initial rumour would ever think there was anything more to it, and if any of the five or six witnesses who had seen the front of my trousers tried to tell their version of the story they'd be accused of exaggeration or told they must have misremembered. By getting ahead of the story and controlling it, I'd be taking what could have been a career-ending moment and turning it into an embarrassing rumour, which could be treated like climate change or the moving of Australia Day and simply ignored. Again, I'm not saying this story is true, but if it was, people might notice a small smile around the corners of my mouth. People might refer to it as a 'perpetual smirk', but those people would be wrong. It would merely be the satisfaction of being the only one who knows the truth.

April 27th 2019

Labor are so upset that I managed to get a preference deal with Clive Palmer and they didn't. They're trying to act like they hate him now, but everyone knows they were begging him to negotiate. Imagine being unable to get a man of Palmer's girth to come to the table. Hashing out a deal with Clive was easy. In exchange for him sending his preferences our way, all we had to promise was to fund the opening of a KFC near his house and agree to let him do literally anything he wants, which, given how rich he is, was pretty much already the case.

April 28th 2019

An interview with Dutton's wife came out in the news today. She said, and I quote, 'He's no monster.' I cannot stop laughing.

April 29th 2019

This evening I came face to face with my enemy when I destroyed Bill in the first Leaders' Debate. I was riding high after yesterday's Newspoll saw me jump another point, putting us at 49-51, levels not seen since early August of last year, so there was no way I was ever losing this debate. I even won the coin toss, so I got to talk first and Bill never recovered. Anything he said, I smiled, telling the viewers at home that this dancing monkey was entirely beneath me.

I'm shocked that he's persisting with his disastrous franking credit policy, though. Sure, people who pay no tax shouldn't get a tax refund, but winning an election is all about how many people you can bribe with pledges of funding and tax cuts. Taking away money people are already getting is like a reverse bribe. Policy can be divided into two camps, pre-election and post-election. Pre-election policy is the shiny stuff, like grants and promising to create jobs, the happy stuff. Post-election policy is the unpopular things that you wheel out once you've been elected and there's enough time for people to forget how angry you've made them before you have to get them to vote for you again. This franking credit thing screams 'post-election', and yet they've been out parading it around like it's the opening of a new hospital. It's just baffling.

I'm assuming the studio audience was stacked with Labor plants due to twenty-five of the forty-eight members saying they thought he won, but I think the real story here is that I managed to move eleven of them to vote 'undecided', and it's even more incredible that I had twelve of them vote for me. To walk away from the debate having turned almost half of the audience plants against their own leader proves just how great at public speaking I really am.

April 30th 2019

I am so glad we decided to get our Queensland hick preferences from Palmer instead of One Nation. Footage just leaked of Steve Dickson, senate candidate and Grand Dragon of One Nation, disgracing himself in an American strip club. His behaviour is disgusting, and I don't want to dignify it by writing it here but it should probably be on record, so I will. He was caught in the same gun rights sting that Pauline was, and hidden cameras recorded him saying some truly abhorrent things and trying to get one of the dancers to touch his willy. It gives me no pleasure to commit this to the annals of history, but the words, 'That young lady has a wonderful set of cahoonas,' will now forever be associated with Steve Dickson, and there's nothing anyone can do to change that. Some members of the National Party thought I was mad when I walked away from a preference deal with the Knights of One Nation, but who's laughing now? The answer is Australia, after hearing Steve Dickson say the word 'titty' on national television.

May 1st 2019

Just remembered Peter's wife saying he's not a monster and had another big laugh. To be fair to her, though, I'd probably say the same thing about my spouse if I'd knowingly married someone sewn together from a bunch of stolen corpses.

May 2nd 2019

The world is certainly a very different place at the moment. I've just had to ask one of my candidates in Tasmania to step down over some old social media posts. This lady,

Jessica Whelan, apparently posted a number of anti-Muslim comments on Facebook, which, in any previous election, would have been fine. With the current political climate, though, these old comments have become unacceptable, and she should have thought about this when she was making them at the time.

What's pissed me off the most about this whole thing isn't that she made the comments, but that when they came to light she told my staff that she hadn't and that the screenshots the press had published were doctored. My staffers then passed this on to me and I defended her, which has made me look like someone who doesn't know when they're being lied to. We can perhaps spin this whole thing into a story about how trusting I am and that I try to see the good in people, but I'd rather be focussing on denigrating Bill Shorten.

It hasn't all been bad news today – a number of other candidates have also been caught out on social media. A One Nation candidate's personal Facebook was found to contain pictures of him groping a woman in Thailand along with a bizarre picture of a naked horse lady with the caption, 'MMMM!!! . . . interesting thoughts'. Aside from *Oh Jesus, why would anybody make this?*, I can't for the life of me imagine what those thoughts could be.

The worst of all, though, came predictably from the Labor camp. Their candidate for Melbourne, Luke Creasey, should never be forgiven for what he has done. Not only did he post links to pornography and make rape jokes, he also wrote what is perhaps the most reprehensible thing I have ever seen on the internet. Not that I would expect anything better from a Melbournite, but that vile creature wrote, 'Endorsement by those who call the Sutherland Shire home is not something that anyone with decency should aspire to.' Now, I'm a man with pretty thick skin. I understand that lefties have no self-control and will attack me based purely on my many victories for the right, but to go after the people of The Shire, the hardest working men and women on the face of the earth, just to try to cheapen my position as their representative, is nothing short of disgusting.

The most black and white of the Ten Commandments is 'Thou shalt not kill', but I'm sure that even God would support bringing back the death penalty for behaviour as low as this. Creasey, as a man, is irredeemable, and were Australia a totalitarian regime he would be rightly sent to the gulag. My outrage was only compounded when Bill Shorten refused to stand him down. I know Bill is on the ropes, but surely, even in his desperation, he can see that Creasey is a lost cause. Why he's sticking his neck out for their candidate for the seat of Melbourne, an electorate so Green it's practically chained to a tree, is beyond me. Well, the second debate is tomorrow, and the gloves are coming off.

May 3rd 2019

Luke Creasey stood down today, but that didn't mean I
went easy on Bill in the debate. At one point I stood over
him, imposing my will, and he panicked like a little boy
being poked in the ribs and called 'Scott no mates' by
the big boys on the bus home from school. I know he's
not good under pressure, but the only thing he could
come up with was calling me a 'classic space invader',
causing everyone in the room to laugh at how terrible an
insult that is. If you're going to try to belittle someone,
comparing them to a hugely popular video game that all
the kids are totally down with is the worst way to go about
it. Any teenager watching that debate would have heard
that and thought, *Space Invader? That's my favourite
video game at the arcade! Scomo must be a total cuck!*
For anyone over the age of 18, 'cuck' is a slang term
similar to 'legend' or 'radical dude', which I deduced from
how many times I was called one by teens on Tweeter.
I did even better in this debate than the last one, managing
to take Bill's planted audience all the way to a result of
'no clear winner'. The final debate won't have an audience
vote to rig, but even without one, I'm still going to beat
him for a third time.

May 4th 2019

I'm incredibly proud of my team. They're mostly lifelong virgins who we take in when they become too old for university politics, but they sure know how to stir up a reaction online. Today is the fourth of May, which is when the movie *Star War* takes place, so they came up with a brilliant campaign image to cut through all the talk of hurt feelings and 'micro-aggressions' on Tweeter. They photo-chopped my head onto the body of the *Star War* guy with the laser sword and captioned it with, 'The economy is strong with this one,' a reference to how good a businessman its director, Steven Spielberg, is. The picture didn't get a lot of 'likes' on Tweeter, but it did attract over a thousand comments, which is known in the world of social media as 'a great ratio'.

I loved seeing myself as the hero of a blockbuster movie and thought it would play very well with the youth, but I didn't think it quite captured the message of our campaign, which is 'Bill Shorten is a hole'. I asked my team if, perhaps, they could come up with something a bit more negative that focussed less on the good things I was doing and more on the bad things Labor were doing, and they really outdid themselves. The new image still drew on the famous *Star War* date, but instead of me in a heroic pose, it had Bill dressed as the villain Dark Vader, with the caption 'Stop Labor's debt star', which is a reference to Dark Vader's spaceship, the Dead Star. This one didn't receive as many likes or comments, but our analytics indicate that a lot of people saw it, which is what's most important. Now when any young person, or a particularly cool person over forty, sees Bill Shorten, they'll be reminded of one of the biggest villains in popular culture, much like how when foreigners see the Bimble lady they think of swearwords and going to Australia for a holiday.

May 5th 2019

I read some of the replies to my *Star War* posts. In unrelated news, I've come up with a new plan to crack down on internet trolls. No ordinary, hard-working Australian should ever be called an 'intergalactic dildo' or 'Emperor F**k-knuckle', and the people doing it need to be heavily punished.

Bill had his campaign launch today. I didn't watch but I'm told Rudd and Gillard sat next to each other. I'm assuming they didn't have microphones anywhere near the audience or all you would have been able to hear was Julia 'reluctantly' talking about her misogyny speech for the nine millionth time and Kevin sulking that she was taking the attention off of his 'regular Aussie bloke' routine. Paul Keating was there too, obviously, as that man will attend the opening of an envelope, although he'd likely only stay long enough to call the envelope 'a brown stain on the jocks of democracy' before leaving.

This is the problem with Labor leaders – they're complete egomaniacs. I mean, look at Shorten. What kind of a man thinks he's worthy of going one on one with an absolute titan of the Liberal Party, hand-picked by God to lead this country into its greatest period of economic success since Federation? The fact that he hasn't pulled the Labor Party out of the race entirely is an act of staggering arrogance.

May 6th 2019

I'm getting real mileage out of a little slogan I came up with after a chance encounter with a man in a service station. It was late on a Friday and I'd just popped in to get a few Magnum Ego ice-creams for my dessert when a rather drunk chap stumbled through the door and grabbed the last chunky beef Traveller pie from the warmer. I was staring at it, regretting not buying it myself, when he saw me looking and said, 'I know. How good are pies.' The drunk refused to hand over the pie, but as I sat in my car, eating the sausage roll I was forced to buy instead, I realised he had given me something much better: a new three-word slogan.

It's been proven that the average Australian brain can only process five words at a time before it forgets what is being said, so the most effective campaign slogans are at or beneath this number. How good is beer! How good are the Sharkies! How good is Australia! This slogan works so well because it is completely adaptable while never really committing to a concrete position. I'm not saying, 'Beer is good.' I'm asking, 'How good is beer?' Sure, the suggestion is there that it's good, but I'm not the one saying it. If someone is an alcoholic whose life has been ruined by beer, I'm just asking a question and they can't hold that against me. But if they're normal, it's a way for them to relate to me, someone they might have thought completely out of their league thanks to all my success. How good is universal popularity!

May 7th 2019

Some absolute loser tried to egg me today. Thankfully it didn't break, but the sentiment has left me furious. I was in Albury (which, being in the country, is a bad enough way to spend the day), asking some old ladies at a CWA meeting if I would be allowed my own personal cake, when a protestor snuck up from behind and hit me over the head with an egg. Thankfully, I have a very soft skull – doctors have compared it to plasticine, as it will hold a thumbprint for several days – so it bounced off, not even breaking when it hit the floor.

It's disgusting she was even there in the first place. Anyone who is that incapable of breaking an egg has no business being at a CWA meeting. I'm assuming she was taking inspiration from the boy who humiliated Anning and, not being from Queensland, took the only opportunity she could to get in the papers when a famous person visited her hometown. The difference between her and Egg Boy, though, is that Egg Boy attacked a universally despised loser while she tried to embarrass a national hero.

I was, however, able to use this situation to my advantage. In the kerfuffle, one of the CWA bints was knocked to the ground and, in full view of the cameras, I helped her up. If I wasn't so close to the end of an election campaign my good-deed instincts might not have been this sharp. I further capitalised on the sorry egging attempt when I drew a comparison between the protestor and a group of vegans who have been invading farms. A vegan probably wouldn't use an egg, but one thing country people love is when they think you're like them, and they'll ignore little inconsistencies as long as it makes them feel normal.

For any other leader this probably would have been enough, but I had one final trick up my sleeve. After suggesting the protestor might be a vegan, I then compared her to the unions as a quick shout-out to my friends back home in the city. Name one other Prime Minister who could be hit with an egg, look like he cares about the elderly, make farmers think he understands why anyone would choose to live in the dirt, and empathise with property developers all in one day. To top it off, the cakes were left unattended in the kitchen afterwards so I was able to grab five to take with me. Admittedly, all that cream has made me feel quite sick, but I'm not going to let that detract from how much of a victory today was.

May 8th 2019
The third and final Leaders' Debate is in the books and, as predicted, Bill absolutely tanked. Perhaps he wouldn't have done so poorly in the face of a lesser adversary, but, to borrow an analogy from my favourite book, this was a classic David and Goliath battle, only this time Goliath (me) won. The most amazing point of the whole debate had to have been when Bill was asked about Labor's franking credits policy. Instead of saying, 'That was a terrible idea

and we've changed our minds,' he went into a long, drawn-out spiel about how 'fair' it was. In his infinite wisdom (this is sarcasm), he even asked which schools would have to be closed to pay for the predicted $8 billion that franking credits are going to cost the budget in future years, as if the people receiving them have any use for a school. Earth to Bill, they're retired! They're way too old to go to school! He keeps calling the credits a 'very generous gift', and he's right, they are a gift – a gift of thousands of votes from Labor to the Liberal Party.

Right near the end of the debate Shorten tried to hit me with a sucker punch when he asked why so many of my ministers were retiring, but once again I was too quick for him. First, I dodged the question with a quick, 'No need to get nasty,' reminding everyone at home of his history as a union bully. Then as he rambled on I followed up with a little trick we used to use in the ad business when a lady would get offended by a bit of racy banter and told him to smile because it was only a joke. Even after this complete humiliation, he still kept going, so I had no choice but to take the gloves off and deliver my knockout blow. I brought up that Kelly O'Dwyer, my lady Minister for Ladies, was retiring to be a housewife so she could spend time with her children, making Bill look like a total sexist. There was no crowd vote to crown a winner, but I could tell by his limp grip and the tears that formed in his eyes as I squeezed the

GOLIATH
AND
DAVID

life out of his hand during our final handshake that he had conceded defeat.

May 9th 2019

A little quote I read from Kristina Keneally today: 'Peter Dutton has been let out of his cave. He's been kept underground somewhere by the Liberal-National party.' First of all, Peter doesn't live in a cave. He lives in a sort of nest made from rotting pieces of meat. These kinds of lies are typical of Labor. I do, however, quite like the idea of keeping Peter underground. I might look into the legality

of it after the election, although we might need to be careful
about how we do it, given the tendency of potatoes to
multiply when buried . . .

May 10ᵗʰ 2019

The Labor Party have finally released their costings. They've
left it until the last minute to avoid scrutiny, but I think the
Australian public are a little smarter than that. According
to their numbers, they've said they're predicting a bigger
surplus than ours, which is just rubbish. The last time
they were in power they inherited their surplus from John
Howard, and what happened? The Global Financial Crisis
hit and they spent it all. Who's to say that, if they're given
another chance at running the country, another GFC won't
hit? They simply can't be trusted with the economy.

Our surplus is going to be achieved specifically because
we're predicting a GFC won't happen, which I haven't heard
the Labor Party mention once in their press conferences
today. Granted, I haven't been listening to them, but I know
what they're like and I'll bet they didn't say a single thing
about planning on having nothing happen to the global
economy. The other bizarre thing about their 'surplus' is that
they intend to achieve it by increasing taxes on the wealthy,
which is campaign suicide as far as I'm concerned. Out of
millionaires and people on welfare, who is more likely to

have control of the media? Why would you try to find your surplus in the bank accounts of the one per cent? They love money, that's why they have so much of it. Do you really think that trying to take that away will result in anything other than them running you out of town? The last person who thought it was a good idea to rob the rich and give to the poor was Robin Hood, and what is he doing now? I'm not entirely sure, it's possible he's dead, but I'll tell you what he's not doing – being Prime Minister of Australia. I am.

May 11th 2019

There's been a lot of controversy swirling around a rugby player by the name of Israel Folau lately. After signing a very lucrative contract that relied on him not posting anything stupid on social media, he put a picture on his Instagram saying that Hell awaits for, among others, drunks, homosexuals, fornicators and thieves. While it's true the Bible backs up this statement, those are also some of rugby's biggest supporters and, as every advertising exec knows, making people hate themselves is only effective if you're trying to sell cosmetics or weight-loss plans.

This whole thing has turned into a big discussion about religious freedom, though, and it's exhausting. Personally, I don't think anyone should be punished, but believing that your neighbours are going to burn for all eternity in the lake of fire and knocking on their door and telling them are two very different things. Churches, like multi-level marketing schemes, thrive on new members, and if you tell an adulterer to give up his mistress, don't expect to see him sitting next to you, wallet in hand, when the collection plate comes around next Sunday. It's just good marketing to stay quiet about things that might upset your customers. If people are going to end up in Hell, that's between them and God, and driving them away before you even get them in the door only hurts the church's bottom line.

Some denominations, like the Catholics, thrive on guilt, but they come from old money, so they can afford to leave a few bucks on the table. For newer churches, though, a little bit of selective preaching can go a long way. I'm told Barnaby Joyce, in particular, is a big fan of sermons on

the Nine Commandments at his local parish. As for Folau, while detrimental to his own cause and in clear breach of the terms of his contract, I don't think he should have lost his job. It just doesn't seem right to expect clear and rational thought from a person whose job involves using his head as a battering ram.

May 12th 2019

Third Newspoll in a row that I haven't gone up. I think it's fairly evident that less than a week out from the election and after all my campaigning, they've been calling the wrong people again. Absolutely useless. I'm tempted to ring Uncle Rupert and give him a piece of my mind, but I don't want him running a mean headline if he gets upset, so I might have to wait until after I've won.

It was with this disappointment in my heart that I had to launch my campaign today. I've been kind of fed up with all the work I'm having to do, and I'll admit, I snapped a little. I pitched my whole campaign to 'the quiet Australians', because everyone needs to shut up and just give me a break. Afterwards, though, when I'd calmed down a bit, I realised that, even in anger, my brilliant brain can't help but come up with winning slogans. 'Quiet Australians' perfectly sums up my supporter base. Sure, Bill is beating me in the polls, but that's because the only people who answer their phones to do surveys are noisy Australians – the ones who can't keep their mouths shut, who jump on Tweeter at every opportunity to shout, 'The Prime Minister pooed his pants!' Even though I don't take it personally, these are not the people who will win us the election. The people who will vote us in are the small business owners, the hard-working mums and dads, the retirees just getting on with their lives and chasing the Australian dream of a thousand dollar rebate from the government.

They say the squeaky wheel gets the grease, but what if, for once, the quiet wheels were rewarded. Wouldn't this country run smoother if, instead of repairing its defective components, we focussed our attention on the bits of the engine that are performing at their best? Why not ply the already working parts with as much grease as we can get our hands on and get them running as fast as possible? Besides, the best way to oil a rusty gear is to apply the lubricant to the gears around it and let the excess trickle down to where it's needed.

May 13th 2019

There have been reports today that Clive Palmer is currently on holiday in Fiji instead of campaigning. I asked the cabinet What's App group if I could maybe vote early and do the same thing because of how hard I've worked, but the only response was from Michaelia Cash, who wrote, 'Don't f**king test me, Scott.' I pretended I was joking to avoid waking up in that pit she has in her basement and being forced to rub lotion on myself, but why shouldn't I go? I've been flying all over the country for a whole month, coming up with bribes to win over the nation, when all they've had to do is wander down to the local shops and promise to put in a new roundabout, or whatever it is that MPs are meant to do for their electorates. It's not fair that I should have to stay here for the whole election campaign without a holiday just because I'm the leader. As soon as this is over, I'm going straight to Fiji.

May 14th 2019

Bill Shorten keeps trying to link my faith to my leadership to get lefties to vote for him. In his latest attack he suggested I might believe gay people go to Hell, which is just an out-and-out lie. I would like to state now, once and for all, that I do not believe people go to Hell for being gay. If you have gay sex, sure – according to the Bible that's a bit of an abomination and you're probably in for some eternal suffering come Judgement Day – but wanting to commit sin and actually *committing* said sin are not the same thing.

The boy next door has been learning the trumpet for the last few months, and, I'll admit, sometimes when he's practising while I'm trying to sleep in on a Saturday morning I'm tempted to break the sixth commandment, but as long as I hold that urge at bay, God has no reason not to let me into Heaven. But none of this has anything to do with running the country. If a man wants to kiss another man and condemn himself to an unrelenting eternity in the lake of fire, that's his business. I may be the most powerful man in the country, but I'm not in charge of the Apocalypse. I don't hold one of the seven trumpets, mate. As I said to a journalist today, 'I'm not running for Pope, I'm running for Prime Minister.' That said, my church doesn't actually have a Pope. It has lasers and electric guitars instead, which are much more exciting.

May 15th 2019

I am very ready for all of this to be over and for Bill Shorten to finally stop his bleating and crawl into his grave. You can tell he's getting desperate now, as he's started falling back on calling me a liar. The minute someone does this, you know they've lost the argument because it means you've been able to bend the truth to your will. The truth is like a wild animal. Once you've tamed it, you can climb on its back and ride it to victory. Some people argue that the truth should be left as it is, free from outside interference, but what would an army be without its cavalry? Who would want to visit the circus if it didn't have any elephants? What kind of person would want a cat for a pet? The only people who rail against domesticating the truth are the ones who are unable to do it, so it's not all too surprising that pretty much every animal liberationist happens to also be a leftie.

May 16ᵗʰ 2019

Bob Hawke just died and my team are panicking. According to them, people will see voting for Bill Shorten the day after tomorrow to be Bob's dying wish. Personally, I think they're wrong. Bob has just been looking at those faulty Newpolls and decided he'd rather roll the dice on the afterlife than wait to see what life under a Shorten Labor government would be like. I wish I'd been able to visit and tell him that they've just been calling the wrong people so he could have been around long enough to see me win ~~150~~ 77 seats. I have a lot of respect for Bob, and the feeling was mutual. He once described me as 'a man with all the appeal of an arse-flavoured lollipop,' which I still don't quite understand but appreciate the sentiment.

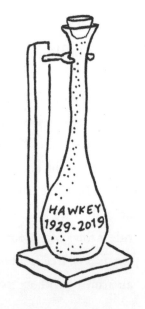

May 17th 2019

It's the day before the election and the final Newspoll of
the campaign just came out. I cannot put into words how
angry I am. We've gone down by half a point! HOW?!
My opponent is Bill Shorten, the human equivalent of wet
bread! What do I have to do? Eff this country and everyone
in it. I hate Australia. After tomorrow I'm quitting politics.

May 18th 2019

I just won the election!!! I mean, I always knew I would, but
the victory still feels good. That creature with the digital
whiteboard they have on the ABC just called 74 seats for the
Coalition and said that, with only 66, he 'can't see Labor
forming government', meaning I smashed Bill!

I've finally worked out what's been going on with
the Newspolls too. Much like God tested Jesus in the
desert, Uncle Rupert has been testing me. I'm happy to
say I passed with flying colours. It's no secret that I am
universally beloved by the good people of Australia, but
what if I wasn't? Only a true leader would be able to hold
it together in the face of the baffling shame of being less
popular than Bill Shorten. Only the kind of Prime Minister
who will be talked about for centuries could have led his
party to victory while the ferals on Tweeter mocked and
jeered. If the Bible was still being written today, this chapter

would, without doubt, be the most popular. I guess, in a way, this diary is kind of a spiritual successor to the Bible – the Book of Scomo. When people look back in two thousand years, I will stand alongside the world's most inspiring names: Moses, Jesus, Napoleon, Donald, Scott. The Mount Rushmore of great leaders. I overcame countless Newspoll losses to snatch victory from the jaws of Bill. I am a hero and I deserve a hero's reward. It's time to start planning my holiday.

May 19th 2019

People are calling my election victory a 'miracle', which I find incredibly offensive. To call it divine intervention completely ignores the hard work I put into winning and how great I am as a leader. Sure, God deserves some of the credit for creating me, but I think at least ninety-five per cent of the praise should go my way. I look at the Big Guy as my running mate, along with the leader of the Nationals (Seamus?), but they are both only supporting roles in the story of Scott. One of the first things a Christian learns is to be humble, so I'm sure God is happy to follow his own rules and allow me to have the spotlight for a little while.

"The Mount Rushmore of great leaders."

May 21st 2019

I've got a problem with one of my election bribes. It doesn't look like we'll be able to recall parliament before the end of the financial year because the numbers from the election won't be finalised, so that big tax rebate can't be passed in time for everyone to get their money when I promised it. I've asked if we can just give the money away without it being passed into law, but my senior advisors have said that loopholes only work if they're 'technically legal' rather than what this is, which is 'completely illegal'.

I think a lot of Australians will be upset that they won't get their money, but this is the sort of thing that happens when the leader of a country isn't given complete control to do whatever he wants without restriction. The food they eat might not be as appealing as sausages or curry, but at least the people of North Korea don't have to wait for Kim Jong-un to push his policy through a hostile senate. There's really nothing I can do while we're waiting on the writs to be returned, so in the meantime I've been planning my holiday.

I've taken inspiration from Clive and decided on Fiji. I wanted to go to Hawaii, but Jenny and the girls said we should go somewhere closer to home, just in case I need to come back early. That's not going to happen, but she said if we go to Fiji this time we can go to Hawaii at Christmas, which I'm happy with because it means I'll get two holidays out of the deal.

May 22nd 2019

Looks like we're on track to win 77 seats, just as I predicted. It would have been more, but the good people of Warringah have decided to punish Tony Abbott for daring to suggest I might lose the election, and rightly so. I've heard that Tony has landed on his feet, though. Using the fact that he looks like an exaggerated caricature of himself to his advantage, he's already begun a lucrative career as a Tony Abbott impersonator. Apparently he's so convincing that people have trouble picking him from a real impersonator.

Fraser Anning has also lost his seat, but I'm assuming he'll just go back to what he was doing before he entered the senate – using a tube to shout directly into his own anus while trying not to attract the attention of any debt collectors.

TONY ABBOTT – TONY ABBOTT IMPERSONATOR

May 26th 2019

Announced my new cabinet today. It's pretty much the
same as the last one, 'cause if it ain't broke, don't fix it, but
I did promote Stuart Robert to Minister for Government
Services and the National Disability Insurance Scheme.
If we're going to get our surplus we need to stop as much
money being bled out of the budget for welfare as possible,
and Stuart was fantastic at protecting the gold in his
previous position as Head Goblin at Gringotts Wizarding
Bank.

May 28th 2019

Today was the first meeting of the party room since the
election, so I needed to make an inspiring speech to really
fire everyone up. It turned out to be pretty easy. I just took
a sermon I heard at church on the weekend, substituted
myself for Jesus and Australians for Christians and, hey
presto, I'm going to 'burn for the Australian people every
single day'. I did have to take Barnaby Joyce aside and tell
him not to take it literally, though. The man really needs
to invest in some SPF 50+ – that sunburn looks like it goes
all the way down to the bone . . .

May 29th 2019

Got sworn in as Prime Minister today. No biggie. I don't want to brag, but this is like my second time or something, so it's not as exciting for me as for some of the new guys, or the Nationals, whose memories only go back about a week due to their rum intake.

May 30th 2019

Albo. They picked Albo to be their leader. And by 'picked' I mean no one bothered to run against him, so he won it by default. This is like if, instead of the Joker, Batman's arch-nemesis was a piece of dry toast. I know there's no one in that party, or mine for that matter, who would pose me any kind of threat, but I was at least expecting them to try.

Now all the almighty Scott Morrison has to defeat at the next election is a man who looks like a sausage in a wig. What a let-down.

June 4th 2019

The press are trying to say it's my fault that the tax cuts won't get passed before the end of the financial year because I chose the date of June 28th for the return of the writs, making any legislation impossible to pass before then. They're also saying, because I agreed to this date when I called the election, that I made my promise of a rebate knowing it was impossible to deliver on time, which just isn't fair to me at all. Even if, deep down, I did know it was impossible when I promised that bribe, I certainly wasn't thinking about it. The only thing I was thinking about was winning the election. Would people rather Bill Shorten was running the country? He wasn't promising any free money! They should just be thankful they're getting anything at all.

Anyway, what's done is done. The writs won't be returned until June 28th, so I've got nothing to do until then except go to Fiji for my holiday. If the electoral commission was better at their job, maybe we could recall parliament sooner, but you can hardly blame me for taking some time away when there's no work for me to do for a month.

June 5th 2019

The press are upset again. They're angry because the AFP raided some lady journalist and the ABC, but then criminals are always angry when their houses get searched, aren't they? Some might be offended by me calling them that, but if they weren't breaking the law then why did they get raided by the federal police?

I'm not bothering with any of that at the moment, though, because today I met the Queen! I'm over in London for the anniversary of the D-Day landings. I only came because I heard Donald was going to be here, but when I was given the chance to meet the woman whose face is on all our money, I had to take it. I gave her one of the presents I was planning on giving Trump, but since I brought him over a whole suitcase full (Jenny had to bring all her clothes as hand luggage), I don't think he'll miss one. It's a signed biography of Australian hero Winx, and I'm told Trump can't or won't read anything over 280 characters anyway. I'm not sure how they got the horse to sign the book, but the Queen said she appreciated it so that's all that matters.

June 10th 2019

Pauline Hanson has come out and said she won't be supporting our tax cuts when we get them to the senate, and honestly, this is great news for me. Now if we can't get the legislation through, we can pin all the blame on One Nation. Xenophobia is already a bit out of fashion at the moment, so racists are the perfect minority to discriminate against.

June 16th 2019

I'm finally in Fiji! We were upgraded to first class on the way over because I'm very important, and when we arrived at the resort they upgraded me again! We're in a luxury villa that comes with a private beach and a butler. My friend Alan has always told me I should have a butler, which he calls a 'boy helper', but I never knew just how good having one could be. I haven't had to get my own beer once! I just clap my hands twice, shout 'Butler!' and he comes running with a stubby of Tooheys New. I feel like Malcolm Turnbull (only not terrible at my job or universally loathed by my colleagues).

June 18th 2019

Why can't the Electoral Commission just do their job properly? They were meant to return the writs on June 28th, but now they're saying they're going to be finished counting early and are estimating a return date of the 24th. This, of course, has got everyone pressuring me to cut my holiday short and recall parliament to pass the legislation in time for the tax office to pass on the cuts. Well, I'm not going to do it. It's not my fault the Electoral Commission can't stick to the dates they were given. I took this holiday on the good faith that there wouldn't be any work to do before July, and I refuse to be punished for that – I've got a free butler, for Christ's sake! Do they expect me to give that up just so some tradie can blow an extra grand on the pokies when he gets his tax return?

June 21st 2019

I've just been informed that the writs have been returned. Not only did they miss the initial date by a week, they also missed their revised date and finished up three days before that! Now the pressure is really on for me to get back and start drafting up the legislation. I've still got three days of my holiday left, so I'm going to turn off my phone.

June 22nd 2019

I got a bit bored with just having my butler bring beers to my hammock, so I decided to take a look at the final election numbers. Doing that preference deal with Clive really paid off. He didn't get a single candidate elected, but his preferences and smear campaign delivered the Coalition an extra five senate seats! Not only that, but One Nation will see two of their senators hanging up their sheets for good, Derryn Hinch will have to go back to naming paedophiles on radio and going to prison for it, and David Leyonhjelm will have to find somewhere other than the Parliament House toilets to cry when people are mean to him. Labor and the Greens, predictably, ended up on exactly the same numbers they had before the election, meaning not only am I better than Malcolm at bringing back votes from the far-right, he was also no better than me at winning votes from the left. I know he's gone from my life forever, but it still feels good to get a victory over him.

June 24th 2019

I'm back home from my holiday and people are already at me to recall parliament to get this legislation passed, but I'm far too busy. I need some time to decompress from my holiday, then I've got to fly to Osaka in a few days to attend the G20. I hope no one tries to come up with a new climate change target while we're there. Apparently Kyoto is just up the road . . .

June 28th 2019

The G20 summit is OK, but I'm a bit disappointed with the food in Japan. I was hoping to eat a lot of sweet-and-sour pork and chicken satay, but I haven't been able to find anything like that here. I've spent my life eating at Asian restaurants, and then I come to Asia and all they're eating is octopus donuts and cabbage pancakes. It's weird. I've been having to fill my pockets with bacon at the breakfast buffet to eat through the day. It's kept me from getting hungry, but I've been attacked by the sniffer dogs at the summit much more than I normally would.

I caught up with Donald for dinner last night and gave him the presents I meant to give him in London at the start of the month. At the time, he said he didn't have room on his jet for a whole suitcase of gifts, but if I brought them to Japan he'd pick through them and find space for the things he liked, which is fair. It also gave me time to get another signed copy of the Winx biography for him. I know he won't read it, but the value of an autographed book isn't in the words inside, it's in the signature on the cover, plus there are some glossy picture pages inside for him to look at.

I pressed Donald on his China tariffs and told him they were hurting our economy a bit, but he said they weren't and that his tariffs were 'the best tariffs' and that Australia was 'winning more than it had ever won before', which was hard to argue with. I feel like the dinner might have been more productive if I didn't have to keep ducking off to the bathroom to eat my pocket bacon, but I still left feeling much better about our economic position. My advisors had told me that the tariffs on China were a detriment to

Australia, but Donald said they're not, so I consider the matter settled.

June 29ᵗʰ 2019

Had a real win today. I managed to convince almost everyone at the G20 to back my plan to crack down on cyber terrorism. We, as a global community, will stand together so that never again will a white supremacist live stream the massacre of innocent people. We say no to bullies and bigots using Tweeter to call an elected Prime Minister a 'balding sack of dogs**t with the personality to match' or 'the warm piss running down the leg of democracy'. Enough is enough, and it's time to come together as leaders of the free world, with perhaps me in charge because it was my idea, and stamp out this outrageous abuse of technology.

June 30ᵗʰ 2019

Today is the last day of the financial year, which means it is now, unfortunately, too late to get the tax-cut legislation through in time for people to see it in their tax returns this year. I'd recall parliament right now if I could, but it takes days to light the beacons used to call the Nationals back to Canberra. I wish we could have got it through on time, but the blame has to lie squarely at the feet of the Electoral

Commission for their incompetent bungling of the dates, and I think the majority of Australians understand that. I've seen a few people saying this is my fault, but electoral law can be very confusing for people with lower IQs, so I don't take it personally.

July 1st 2019

Why isn't there a Gold Logie for best Prime Minister? I'm way more entertaining than that mean ginger bloke and you don't have to run the risk of being brainwashed by communists, because I'm on more channels than just the ABC. The only show on the ABC I actually enjoy is that *Mad as Hell* with Shaun Micallef. The way they used to make fun of Bill Shorten was priceless and the cast are all spectacular. All except for the little fat boy, Toss Greenslave I think his name is. I don't know why, but there's just something about him that I don't trust. He seems like the kind of person who would make up a bunch of stories just to make fun of someone. Plus, he looks terrible in profile. Like a rat crossed with a fish.

July 4th 2019

My tax cuts passed the senate today, way ahead of schedule. We've only been back for three days and I've already got them through. I think it says a lot about me as a leader that I managed to pass the legislation so quickly, despite all the AEC's fumbling. Now that they've passed into law, anyone who hasn't done their tax return yet can get to it and receive their well-earned bribe. I think it's pretty telling that Labor practically waved the legislation through, with only their left faction, the Greens, standing against it. I said to Mathias that this is the first bill Labor have supported that went well for them, but I don't think he got the joke. It took me at least a month to teach him to do a thumbs up, so laughter is going to take a while.

July 8th 2019

We just paid $750,000 for Bob Hawke's childhood home. Even if he was a Labor Prime Minister, I still think we need to pay our respects to the former leaders of this country. Plus, we were able to negatively gear it, so if the budget needs a bit of a boost in ten or fifteen years we can sell it off to a developer for a tidy profit.

July 9th 2019

My friend Brian invited me along to a God concert his church was putting on in Sydney tonight. They have a great set-up, lots of flashy lights and a smoke machine, that really get across the message that Jesus is a magical space wizard who totally rocks. Brian's done a fantastic job with the church since he took over. He got in a bit of trouble during the royal commission because it turned out he didn't tell anyone when he found out his father was a paedophile, but he has since attempted to make up for this error of judgement by making friends with big American

celebrities, like the pop star Justin Beaver and that one off the new Jurassic Park movie. I promised to introduce him to my famous friends if he would introduce me to his, so the next time Trump is in town I'm going to take him out to Brian's church. I'm told Donald is a big fan of flashing lights and sparkly things so he should really enjoy it.

July 13th 2019

Donald invited me over to his house!! In two months he's throwing a big dinner for me at the White House and he said I can even bring some friends, or as the Americans call it, a 'delegation'. This is the first time an Australian Prime Minister has been invited to dinner at the President's since

John Howard over ten years ago, which shows just how much Trump likes me as a friend. Within a couple of hours of announcing the invitation, Brian called me up and asked if he could come. He said he was happy to pay his own way, as his church is a millionaire, but that he needed to be there so he could 'exert my influence at the highest level'. I told him that as long as he could set up a meeting with Justin Beaver or one of the MMMBop brothers, I'd see what I could do.

July 16th 2019

Someone's let slip to Pauline Hanson that people won't be allowed to climb all over Ayers Rock in three months and now she's desperate to keep it open, despite never having climbed it in the sixty-five years she's lived in this country. She's spent all morning going on the breakfast TV shows that got her re-elected, making a plan to do the climb before it closes in October. Personally, I couldn't think of anything worse than dragging myself up a big rock that a bunch of tourists have shat on, but I guess scarcity creates demand. It's like how everyone wanted that Caramilk chocolate because it was hard to find, even though it tastes a bit like a tub of yoghurt that someone's been sick in.

July 19ᵗʰ 2019

What a horrible day. I had to meet with Jacinda Ardern and, like a broken record, she started talking about the whole deportation thing again. It took a full hour of me nodding my head and saying 'yup' and 'we'll look into it' for her to shut up. Further to this, after Jenny and I gave her a present for her daughter that my staffers had thoughtfully picked out, she had the gall to admit she hadn't brought me anything in return. At the very least she could have picked up a big Toblerone at duty-free on the way in. To add insult to injury, she then overstayed the twelve-hour visa I had Peter issue her, when her plane broke down. I offered to have some of our guys fix it but she said it would need an engineer from New Zealand, since the Australian ones don't know how to work with wood.

July 20ᵗʰ 2019

Melbourne City Council just declared a climate emergency, which is typical coming from the state that only exists because New South Wales farted. I'm assuming, being Melbourne, that the emergency is centred around how God-awful the weather is down there. I'm not sure what a council is going to do about climate change, though. Maybe they'll replace their garbage trucks with bicycles or only give planning permission to wind turbines . . .

July 23rd 2019

That dork who tried to egg me during the election was
sentenced today. She only ended up with 150 hours of
community service, but I don't hold that against the judge.
Our jails only have so much space and, sadly, they're not
allowed to sentence people to time in the stocks anymore.
I hope that a few weeks picking up rubbish teaches this
young lady that, while it might be OK to smash an egg on
the head of a political toadstool like Fraser Anning, trying
to do the same to the Prime Minister is not OK. Do what
you want to everyone else, but I'm off limits.

July 27th 2019

I don't know why big rock bands say they get tired of
playing their hits. I love it! I flew in to WA today for the
Liberal State Conference, played a tight twenty-minute set
of my best Bill Shorten gear and the crowd lapped it up. It
was so nice to be able to attack Bill again. I've been missing
making fun of him since he retired as leader, and going after
Albo feels like trying to wrestle a fart. After my speech I did
the only other thing worth coming to Perth for and drank
an Emu Export on Cottesloe Beach then wandered up to the
nude bit to try to see some boobs before getting in my plane
and heading home.

July 28ᵗʰ 2019

The first Newspoll since the election was published today and it looks like my theory about Uncle Rupert testing me was correct. It's still not as accurate as I would have expected, but I'm finally on top! We're beating Labor 53 to 47! This is also great news for me because it means that people didn't just like me more than Bill, they like me more than anyone chosen to lead the Labor Party. I can't even remember the last positive Newspoll for the Liberal Party, but I assume it was back when Howard was in, so it makes sense that I, his worthy successor, would be the one to not only bring the budget back into the black, but also the party's popularity.

August 1ˢᵗ 2019

Today is the tenth sitting day since the election and I am exhausted. I can't wait for the winter break to start tomorrow. It runs all the way until the 8ᵗʰ of September and will finally give us all a well-earned break. I think I'll use this downtime to start planning my next holiday. There's another six weeks of sitting days between now and the end of the year, so when Christmas finally rolls around some time on the beach will be long overdue.

August 2nd 2019

A friend of mine, Andrew Bolt, has gotten into another
fight with a child. It's a fairly regular occurrence for him,
but it's normally over wanting to use the slide at the local
playground and not with someone with an international
profile. The child in question is Greta Thunberg, a little
girl from Norway or France or something, who has gained
a huge amount of fame for her work on climate change.
Normally Andrew wouldn't go after someone like Greta
because she isn't employed by the ABC, but the fact that
she's managed to meet with a number of lefty world leaders

has really riled him up. He called me in tears, begging me to send one of our submarines to torpedo the yacht she's about to sail to the UN summit in New York. I told him that I was fine with trying to wind back Australia's discrimination laws so he could get back to racially vilifying people, but obliterating a teenage girl was pushing things a bit too far. Besides, the Collins-class breaks if you get water on it, and it would cost far too much to replace one. He threatened me with an attack piece on his Sky News show, but having seen the ratings, I'm not terribly worried.

August 6th 2019

Australia just won a game of cricket over England, which is great news for me. I've never found cricket terribly interesting – they just stand around trying to catch a ball for three days and no one gets bashed up, but polling has revealed that Australians respond very well to the defeat of foreigners. It's why Prime Ministers do so well in wartime. As the old saying goes, war is just sport with tanks and machine guns. I feel like I'd enjoy cricket a lot more if they shot at each other, but it's a very old game so it's probably too late to change the rules.

August 11ᵗʰ 2019

Wealthy paedophile Jeffrey Epstein has been found dead
in jail. It really proves how remorseful he must have felt,
because not only did he severely beat and strangle himself
to death, his body, presumably still moving like a chicken
with its head cut off, managed to make a noose from a
sheet and hang itself after he died. I sent a bunch of flowers
to the White House with a sympathy card. Even though
I never met him and, in my opinion, Epstein was a stain on
humanity whose name will stand alongside the very worst of
history, I still care about Donald and it's never nice when a
friend dies.

August 14ᵗʰ 2019

I'm in Tuvalu for the Pacific Islands Forum, and what should
have been a nice few days on the beach, interspersed with
a couple of chats about 'strengthening ties', has turned into a
massive pile-on. Everyone is attacking me over Australia's
climate change policy, saying I'm not doing enough to
support the region. I know exactly who's behind all this too:
bloody Jacinda Ardern. Just because her country is tiny and
contributes nothing to global warming due to its lack of
electricity, she thinks she can run around behind my back,
reminding all the Pacific leaders that they're in a similar boat.
Or at least they will be when their countries are underwater.

Well, in case anyone hasn't noticed, I'm the leader of *Australia*, not Kiribati or Tuvalu or whatever other ones there are, so my responsibility is to the Australian people. When New Zealand starts taking in one of our products to the extent that China and India buy our coal, then we can talk – and no, criminals with NZ passports don't count. Until these micronations learn to pull their weight and start propping up our economy, though, we have to go to where the money is, and if China wants to bulk-buy old CFC-filled fridges from us so they can cut them open to use in their ozone depletion program, then who are we to refuse? Buying a few cases of Crown Lager for Aussie tourists to drink doesn't make you a major trading partner, unfortunately.

August 15th 2019

Jacinda and her mates had another dig at me today. They're upset because Australia is using carryover credits from the Kyoto Protocol to meet its emissions targets. We earned those credits! Do they want us to just give them up? If you ask someone to do the dishes once a week for a month and they wash them four times in the first week, they should be allowed to take the rest of that month off. Sure, dirty crockery might pile up over the subsequent three weeks, but simple maths has proven that they have met their obligations. To ask them to clean up again would be unfair.

A person shouldn't be punished for being efficient and finishing their work early, and I refuse to let our country be hit with a sentence that doesn't take into account time already served.

August 17th 2019

My friend Alan Jones is in hot water for saying on his radio program that I should stick a sock down Jacinda Ardern's throat. A lot of people who don't listen to his show have been campaigning for advertisers to pull their support, which I think is counterintuitive. This is bad for Jones, sure, as the majority of what he says when he does talk is paid advertising, and you can only call for race riots for so long before one actually happens and you get in trouble, but it's also bad for his detractors – fewer ads means more Alan. Ads make up a good seventy per cent of the three and a half hours Alan spends on air every morning, and by removing them you just give him more time to speak. I think everyone should take a step back and cool off. Alan may have gone too far in suggesting that I assault the Prime Minister of New Zealand with a sock, but, as usual, his heart was in the right place and I think we can all agree that a little bit of shoosh from Jacinda probably wouldn't go astray.

August 18ᵗʰ 2019

Jacinda must have been in the ear of the leader of Fiji, Frank
Bananarama, because he's just come out and said he doesn't
consider me a friend anymore, calling me 'very insulting and
condescending'. I find this incredibly rude, as it comes after
my deputy (pretty sure his name is either Andy or Alasdair)
reinforced our commitment to keep bringing over Fijians
to pick our fruit, even if their country becomes so flooded
they can't live there. They will, of course, have to build some
sort of giant, floating raft to return to, as their working
visas are only temporary and fruit doesn't need to be picked
year-round, but that could be a real help to them when they
don't have tourists to look after anymore. This is what you
get for trying to be nice to people. Oh well, I guess I'll just
have to have all of my holidays on other islands from now
on. Their loss.

August 23ʳᵈ 2019

Barnaby Joyce is threatening to move to the crossbench
if people don't stop being mean to him over his
attempts to interfere in New South Wales state matters.
Gladys Berejkjijkjkjijln's government is debating the
decriminalisation of abortion and Barnaby is trying his best
to persuade them not to. I think we're safe if he does defect,
though. All that sun looks to have finally boiled his brain

and he's forgotten he's a federal politician, so if he did leave the Nationals he'd most likely end up on the crossbench of state parliament instead of ours, and it would be Gladys who'd have to negotiate with him.

August 24th 2019

I'm currently in France for the G7 summit. Australia isn't normally invited but I texted Donald that I wanted to come along and watch, so he pulled some strings. Today is also the one-year anniversary of my Prime Ministership! I can't believe just how much I've achieved in a single year. I'd write it all down but I'm so busy with meetings that I don't have the time.

August 25th 2019

Pauline got stuck halfway up Ayers Rock and had to come back down. The best part is she took a camera crew with her, so we can all watch it over and over again. As usual, I'm not entirely sure what her point was, but it now seems to be that the climb shouldn't be closed just because it's offensive to Aboriginal people, but because it's also too dangerous, but people *should* still be allowed to climb the rock because it's our right, so it should stay open, but if someone dies Pauline warned us that it was going to

kill someone and it never should have been open in the
first place.

I managed to get a twenty-minute meeting with
Donald at the summit today, even though his schedule was
supposedly full. All the conference rooms were booked out,
so we had to have it in the hallway, but he told me all about
how he's going to turn the G7 into the G8 again by bringing
Russia back in, and that he's going to 'Nuke the balls off
Iran'. I asked if maybe we could change it into the G9 by
adding Australia too, but he said he was out of time and had
to get to McDonald's for his lunch.

I also invited all the world leaders to come with me for
a swim tomorrow morning, to try to make friends with

the ones I hadn't met yet. The president of Chile, Sebastian Pinata, was particularly interested, saying that, looking at me, he was surprised I did any exercise at all. I told him that looks can be deceiving and in my youth I had been known to regularly swim a whole lap at my local indoor swimming pool.

August 26th 2019

I had a great chat with Boris Johnson from the UK this evening. He was particularly excited to show me a diploma he'd recently received from someone he referred to as 'The Wizard' and how it made him a 'Doctor of Thinkology'. I asked him if he could commit to a trade deal with Australia once Brexit goes through and he said he thought it was a great idea, as our coal will be very appealing to their citizens after a couple of months of only having access to British food.

August 27th 2019

Everyone keeps stirring me up because I said my favourite superhero is Aquaman. I was doing an interview for a kids show called *Behind the News* when they hit me with a really tricky question out of left field. I'd gone in with a solid plan on how to step around questions about climate change, which seems to be the only thing young people are interested in these days. It's even more popular than that Chinese cartoon Poker Mons used to be. They can't get enough of it. What I didn't know at the time was that this show was on the ABC – the most underhanded, biased news service in the country. If I'd known beforehand, I never would have agreed to take part. These little snots had probably been undergoing extensive interrogation training from Leigh bloody Sales, and I walked in with a smile on my face, oblivious to how unfairly they were about to treat me.

Every journalist knows that if you are about to interview a world leader it is only polite that you stick to the talking points their office has provided you in advance. People like Sales don't care about politeness, though. All they care about is digging around for 'scoops' and forcing you to tell the truth without regard to how it might make you look to the public. A respectable journalist like David Koch understands this. His breakfast television program, *Today*, is a prime example of how entertaining and informative an interview can be if you ask the questions your guest has prepared answers for.

I will say, though, if ever given the opportunity, try to do your interviews with Koch via satellite. If you go into the studio, he will corner you in your dressing room and read gags from his joke book for hours. It's the reason that, since coming back to politics, Pauline Hanson now speaks like she's on the verge of tears. I think if you asked her she'd say it was worth it, since David and his lady journalist co-host Sam helped drive her re-election campaign. I do not resent them for this, since Pauline will normally vote our legislation through the senate in exchange for being allowed to eat all the Orange Slices from the Family Assorted tray in the upper-house tearoom.

These children were nothing like David Koch. While they did give me a question on climate change and let me talk about my favourite place in the world, The Shire, they also asked about things like anxiety, which I have never experienced, and what job I would do if I wasn't Prime Minister – as if the position of Chief Marketing Officer doesn't exist in private companies. It was one of the last few questions that really got my bile up, though. They asked me who my favourite superhero was. I've been advised not to talk too much about religion so the real answer, Jesus, was out. Instead I'd have to find a fictional superhero and just pretend to like him. I'm not too big to admit that I panicked a bit and just said the first one I could think of, which was Aquaman. If I had the chance to answer again, I'd probably pick Superman. He has lasers for eyes, is virtually indestructible and is the boss of the Justice League. He's essentially a fictional version of me. Aquaman can talk to fish. That's it. Sure, I've had a number of conversations with Gerard Henderson, but I'd hardly consider that a superpower. I mean, Andrew Bolt does it all the time, so it can't be that hard.

August 29th 2019

I'm home in Australia again and getting back to the important task of running the country. I was told on the radio today that, in my absence, someone has put up signs at Parliament House telling people to use whichever toilet suits their gender preference, and talkback radio listeners are outraged. Being a man of the people, I promised to do everything in my power to get those signs taken down, even if it meant going all the way to the top and having someone in my office do it for me.

Personally, I don't care if people want to get sex changes or identify as another gender to use the other

toilet, but putting up a sign that says it's OK crosses the line into PC Tweeter lefty territory and I simply cannot abide it. If one of our voters visits parliament and sees us openly embracing people's gender identities and letting them freely use the toilets as they please, then that voter will no longer be ours. If there's one thing that scares our voter base more than anything – more than even the housing market crashing – it's that someone might pretend to be the opposite gender to listen to a lady wee or see a man's willy.

August 30th 2019

People are calling on me to protect some family in Queensland from being deported, as if immigration is my job. There's a reason I put Dutton in charge of all that stuff. It allows me to maintain a hard-line refugee policy while laying the nastier realities of what that entails at the feet of my main rival, lest the Tweeter luvvies get it into their heads that he's one of them because he put a leather jacket on and start saying, 'It's on,' until a spill happens. Peter has said he's sending them to Christmas Island for some reason. I'd ask why, but the answer would just be the same as it always is with him: 'I like to hurt people.'

September 3rd 2019

I've had to put a stop to all of this talk about me stepping in and saying this Biloela family can stay in Australia. I simply will not do it. If they wanted me to help them then they should have paid $10,000 for a ticket to the Liberal Party's Australian Business Network fundraiser at Channel 9 studios last night and asked me in person like everyone else who wants me to do them a favour.

September 8th 2019

Now Albo has decided to chime in on this family . . . If he wants them to stay so badly, he can get elected in three years, make himself Minister for Immigration and give them all citizenship. Until then he needs to shut up and stop taking the attention off the fact that I'm going to Donald's house in two weeks!

Outside of Canberra, there have been a couple of out-of-control bushfires in Queensland and New South Wales. Seems very early for those to start, but I guess that's what happens when you've had years of drought caused by, I assume, Labor mismanagement. Glad it's a state issue, though. I'd hate for that to be my job – and not in a pretend way, like when Tony used to dress up as a fireman and ride around in the truck making the siren noises with his mouth. I've sent a message to the premiers letting them know that, in these trying times, they are not only in my thoughts, but my prayers as well.

September 9th 2019

Back to work today for a marathon stretch of sitting days. I won't get another break now until I leave to visit Donald in America, which is two whole weeks away. Some people have said that the Prime Minister's salary of $550,000 a year is too high, but I tell you what, I earn every cent of that pay cheque.

September 11th 2019

Sometimes I think Labor just push back on my ideas for the sake of it. We're trying to get legislation through at the moment that would trial the requirement of welfare recipients to be drug tested, and Albo has been jumping up and down, calling it demeaning and cruel. If he can think of a better way to claw back a bit of money to plump up our surplus I'd like to hear it! Setting aside the fact that drugs are illegal, they're also quite expensive. Since dole payments are affected by outside earnings, we know that if someone tests positive for drugs they must be doing cash-in-hand work or getting money from somewhere else, since the paltry amount Centrelink pays them is nowhere near enough to buy something like cocaine, which, according to my friends in the advertising industry, is very expensive.

We're also trying to introduce a welfare card along with this legislation that would prevent people on the dole from spending those payments on alcohol and gambling. The government gives these people just enough, in most cases, to survive. I think most Australians would be pretty upset if they knew they could take this money down to the casino and turn it into a million dollars.

One of the key values of Australia is the fair go, but that fairness has to cut both ways, and the only free money from the government that should be spent on luxuries like beer and poker machines is the tax rebates we give to people who work. If a man without a job is allowed to spend his money on the same things as a small business owner who works sixty hours a week to support his family, then where is the incentive for him to ever find employment? If second class doesn't exist, then there's nothing special about being in first.

September 18th 2019

The past week has really dragged. I've been in parliament the whole time, but I couldn't tell you what was discussed because my mind has been on bigger things. I fly to America tomorrow for a whole week with my best friend in the world, Donald Trump. I am so excited to spend eight days fully embracing the American way of life – eating hamburgers, driving on the wrong side of the road and shooting machine guns. I hope I can get to sleep tonight!

September 19th 2019

I've just landed in America to find out that Australia has been taken off the list of speakers at the UN Climate Change Summit on the 23rd because of our support for coal. I'm kind of relieved, if I'm honest. I could not think of anything more boring than listening to that Greta Thunberg speak while nodding my head and pretending I think our economy is less important than the temperature going up by a couple of degrees. This also frees up one of my days in America to do something fun. Maybe I'll go to Disneyland.

September 20th 2019

I just had the best night of my life! When we got to the White House, I was treated like a king and Jenny was treated like someone who had just arrived at a state dinner with a king. For dinner we were served fish and vegetables, which, if I'm perfectly honest, didn't look incredibly appealing, but Donald noticed and took me aside into what he calls his 'hamberder room', which is a fully staffed McDonald's hidden behind a bookcase, the name of which he has changed, in a very clever play on words, to McTrump.

He said he got the idea from his favourite movie, *Richie Rich*, and it was the first modification he made to the building since he moved in. He also had a giant slide built, and installed a movie theatre and a catapult that has been modified to fire children. I said the girls would love to have a go on that if we came back, but he told me that it wasn't a toy and was only to be used as a defence mechanism if the secret service ran out of bullets and they had to use the staff as ammunition to protect him.

He apologised for not letting my friend Brian come, but I told him it was fine – I'm not really that close with him anyway. After our hamberders, Trump took me to the Oval Office and I watched him go on Tweeter for a few hours before it was time to go home. When I found Jenny, she asked where I'd been and why I'd left her with Melania for so long. Apparently it had been very difficult to talk to her because she kept switching out with a series of body doubles, so they had to constantly restart the conversation. When I told her how much of a great night I'd had, though, she said, 'Well, as long as you're happy, I guess no one else matters,' which was very kind of her.

September 21st 2019

Today Donald and I announced plans for Australia to give America $150 million to help them get to the moon. After that they're going to head to Mars, but Trump said he wanted to do the moon first because the original landings were 'fake news'. I had been a little dubious of the whole fake news thing, but then I won an election after months of people telling me I was unpopular with the Australian public, so it definitely exists. Donald told me that as a reward for Australia's generous donation to his lunar mission he's got a really exciting day planned for me and Jenny tomorrow. He said he just *knows* we're going to love it. Can't wait to find out what we'll be doing.

September 22nd 2019

Donald's surprise was taking us to a cardboard box factory. He said he thought I would like it because it was run by Anthony Pratt, who is an Australian. Personally, I loved it. It was a very generous gesture for Donald to fly us all the way out to Ohio to see the box factory – I'd never been inside one before! Jenny, on the other hand, was less enthusiastic. She said that tomorrow needs to be really special or she's going home early because she 'didn't fly halfway around the world to watch cardboard get recycled with a blithering geriatric in an adult nappy'. I'm not sure which one in particular she was referring to, but I didn't want to push it.

September 23rd 2019

Boy did the UN do me a favour by saying I didn't have to attend that climate summit. Apparently Greta Thunberg kicked off and chewed them all out for not doing enough. So much for *Australia* not pulling their weight. According to her, none of them are any better, so as far as I'm concerned they're all a bunch of hypocrites and I won't listen to another word they say. Instead of being scolded by a small European teenager in a sailboat, I took Jenny to visit a factory where they're developing new screens for McDonald's drive-throughs. I told her I'd secured tickets to the hottest show in Chicago, and her face lit up as she started talking about something called *Hamilton*. I had to tell her, no, we were going to spend the day exploring the exciting world of future drive-through technology and that, if we were lucky, we might even get to test it out by ordering a few hamburgers and some apple pies. She looked a little disappointed, but then she said, 'After what I told you yesterday, it's just bloody unbelievable you would take me here,' which I took to mean I'd done a good job and had made up for the whole box factory thing.

September 24th 2019

I'm supposed to speak in front of the UN General Assembly tomorrow and was looking forward to addressing Australia's exclusion from the climate summit and talking about everything we're doing to fight global warming. I've just seen a transcript of Thunberg's speech though, and now I'm in a mad rush to rewrite mine so it doesn't start with the words, 'How dare you?'

September 25ᵗʰ 2019

I nailed my speech today. I was particularly proud of a little moment at the end where I subtly referenced my winning 'quiet Australians' slogan. I wrapped up my speech with 'We must let our children be children,' which is a reference to the old adage that 'Children should be seen and not heard,' and a clever way of telling Greta's parents to shut her up. By saying I'm concerned about her anxiety, I can effectively reframe the reason for what Thunberg is saying from climate change to her parents not doing a good enough job of keeping her happy. A teenage girl should be playing Super Nintendo and talking to boys on the telephone, not sailing yachts to America to shout at world leaders. The real tragedy here is not that the world Greta grows up to inherit might be a burning hellscape of fire and famine, it's that she's not out riding her bike with her friends while it isn't.

September 26ᵗʰ 2019

I thought I had one more day in America with Donald, but because of time zones you lose a day, meaning I'm now on a plane back home and I didn't even get to say goodbye. Jenny must have sensed how upset I am because she's giving me some distance by sitting at the other end of the plane and not talking to me.

October 5th 2019

I spent the day down in Tasmania addressing the Liberal State Council. I made sure to talk as much as I could about Australia's economy as, while the island still operates on a barter system, it's important for them to know that, one day, with enough hard work and genetic evolution, they might have an economy of their own and be able to export resources other than just chocolate and beer.

October 8th 2019

An environmental group have started sitting on roads around the country to protest climate change by making everyone late for work. I'm glad they've chosen a 'piss everyone off' approach instead of the usual 'just piss Scott off' one, because everyone can finally see how exhausting it is to deal with greenies. According to reports, the reason they're doing all this is to 'ensure a world that can sustain human life'. Well, I want an economy that can sustain human life, specifically big business owners who can donate to the Liberal Party to keep dangerous men like Bill Shorten and Anthony Albanese out of power. What these kids don't seem to realise is that without a booming economy, their two-degree cooler world would be utterly dreadful to live in. What's the point in being able to leave the house in summer if you can't afford to buy an ice-cream while you're out there?

October 11th 2019

I got my revenge on the leader of Fiji, Frank Benihana, for saying we weren't friends anymore. I didn't take it personally when he said it, as he must be under a lot of pressure given his country is about to become the new Atlantis, but he still needed to learn his lesson, and what better way than by having the Prime Minister's XIII absolutely decimate the Fijian team in a friendly game of rugby league. I even ran the water out to the players, just to show Frank that not only was I responsible for bringing the players together, I was also part of the team, and this victory was just as much mine as it was theirs. After the match, Benihana looked suitably chastened and ashamed, so I consider the matter settled and our friendship back on track.

October 14th 2019

We've officially announced a big celebrity signing for the government. Scott Cam, who shouts at people on *The Block*, has agreed to be our national careers ambassador for the bargain price of just under $350,000, which is way less than it cost us to get Sonia Kruger to spruik our immigration policy. It will add a real legitimacy to vocational training, especially as it will let kids know that even if you only go to TAFE, you could still end up a big TV star instead of being working class forever. It is also a good way of getting the message out there that wearing hi-vis doesn't have to lead to joining a union, and that tradesmen can still go on to become small business-owning Liberal supporters instead of just communist thugs.

October 15th 2019

Labor are playing politics again. They're trying to take away from my fantastic success in stopping the boats by saying that nearly 100,000 asylum seekers have arrived by plane since the Liberals took power, which is almost double the amount of boat arrivals under the Rudd-Gillard-Rudd government. What I want to know is if they're so concerned about refugees flying into the country, why did they pass the medevac legislation? Only one party is currently trying to get that bill repealed to stop those plane arrivals, and it's not Labor.

October 21st 2019

The press keep asking my office if Brian was invited to my special dinner at the White House. Apparently he's been going around telling people he was invited but didn't want to go, but I don't want to publicly embarrass him because his church has a lot of money that they could donate to us at the next election. This behaviour is quite unusual for Brian, as he's normally very good at keeping secrets.

October 22nd 2019

That blackface-wearing ponce from Canada just won another election, proving once and for all that the United States is the only country in North America worth mentioning. I think it's the height of hypocrisy that I get attacked constantly for my love of fossil fuels, while the Left fall at the feet of a guy who presides over a country that digs oil out of sand and drinks the blood of trees. It's probably because he's a hunk. People can be attractive in a lot of different ways, and I'm told that my good polo shirts have a lot of female fans around Australia, but I don't think it's right for a world leader to have rippling abs. If you're spending that much time doing sit-ups, you're clearly not paying enough attention to running the country. I know that seventy per cent of the population are trapped in their houses by snow for most of the year, so there's less country to actually run, but my point still stands. I don't care if he's been voted prom king for fifteen years running, I think it's highly inappropriate to constantly suggest that all the girl leaders do a vote on 'which boy leader is the most handsome' at the G20. Donald's plan to annex the Great White North cannot happen soon enough.

October 23rd 2019

Labor have reached a new low. They've just referred Angus Taylor to the police to investigate some supposedly doctored documents that he used for an everyday political attack on Sydney Mayor Clover Moore. He provided the press with a report saying Moore had spent $15 million on travel in a single year when the real figure turned out to be less than two per cent of that. Angus said he downloaded the documents from the City of Sydney website, but their metadata showed that those figures have never existed on those documents. It doesn't look especially good, but even if Angus is responsible, which I'm not saying he is, messing up some numbers on a document is not a police matter. It's something we deal with in-house, like overclaiming travel entitlements or forgetting to declare ownership of a few houses. All that was required was a quiet correction and an apology, but now they've got hardworking police officers, men and women who should be out there protecting us from murderers and burglars, investigating an administrative error. Disgusting. The fact that Albo has decided to play this dirty is proof of just how desperate they are now.

October 28th 2019

I'm copping some flak because I didn't attend the closing of the Ayers Rock climb over the weekend. I don't get it!

They closed the climb because they were sick of white people crawling all over it, then they get upset when a white person doesn't turn up. I'm fully supportive of them closing it – I wouldn't want people urinating on the roof of my church and leaving Roll-ups wrappers up there – but you can't have it both ways. Either you want me there or you don't. Telling me that 'context matters' is just sending mixed messages.

October 31st 2019

They've just cancelled this year's APEC summit in Chile due to violent protests, meaning now I won't get to hang out with Donald next month. I wish these protestors would think of others for once in their lives. Here in Australia we've just seen weeks of green protests on climate change and I'm fed up. If a man is able to become best friends with a billionaire television celebrity and leader of the Free World, he should not be prevented from spending time with him just because some dirty socialist decides to hold a parade about a tree or the cost of living or whatever else it is they can't stop whining about. I am furious.

November 2nd 2019

I have had it with these greenies and their 'activism'. I'm currently trying to make it illegal for a person to boycott a business just because it has a connection with a company that makes its money by harming the environment. My staff have said it's not possible to prosecute a person for choosing not to spend their money on a particular product. This country was founded as a prison colony, so surely there's something in the constitution that lets me do whatever I want to my citizens. These leftist creeps need to be punished for stopping me from catching up with my friend.

November 4th 2019

I made a major trade breakthrough at the ASEAN summit today. China have pledged to continue burning everything we send them. Coal, old tyres, unsold leaded petrol – they've said if we can ship it, they can burn it. They've also said that Donald's tariffs won't have any effect on the amount of cheap electronics they manufacture for us, and when we're done with them in a few years, they'll burn those too. This is what running an economy is all about – making deals and ensuring that bucketloads of cash flow in and out of the bank accounts of big business owners. I also got a few tips on how to deal with protestors, but according to my advisors they constitute 'crimes against humanity' and might cause an international incident.

November 7th 2019

Tonight was Tony Abbott's memorial dinner, and it was a fantastic evening. He's not dead or anything, but it was a little bit like a funeral in that it's probably the last time any of us are going to see him again. Alan Jones was the MC but, mercifully, they managed to keep him down to only five songs. I like Alan, but the man has a singing voice like a person being fed through a woodchipper, which, incidentally, is exactly how Alan dealt with the person who leaked those tapes of him swearing at colleagues back in 2004.

Abbott must be doing some sort of program where one of the steps is apologising to people, because he was very nice to me during his speech, saying that I saved the Liberal Party and he and Malcolm owe me an enormous debt. None of this is news to me, but it was nice to hear it coming out of someone else's mouth for a change.

All in all I had a wonderful time at the party and the beer and wine flowed freely. Dutton made a joke about how all the alcohol we were drinking could put out the bushfires in

Queensland and New South Wales, which are, at this point, probably too big to contain. It was a surprisingly good joke, but it drew my mind to all the work I'll have coming up because of them. As everyone knows, bushfires are a state issue, but the amount of thoughts and prayers I'll have to give over the coming summer is really going to tucker me out, not to mention the two weeks of work we still have to get through before the end of the year. At least I have my holiday to look forward to.

November 11th 2019

Today was a pretty heavy day. It's not my job, but sometimes a leader has to pitch in and help, even if it's a state issue, so I went out to give some hope to the survivors of these tragic bushfires. The one thing that always cheers me up when I'm feeling a bit down is meeting a celebrity, and what bigger celebrity is there than someone who's on television almost every day – the Prime Minister of Australia. I spent the day finding people who had lost their houses and giving them all a comforting handshake. It's not going to bring back their homes, but in twenty years they'll be able to look back on this day and remember that they shook hands with the most famous man in the country, which is pretty bloody special.

November 13th 2019

Some really nasty politics is being played over these fires at the moment. The Greens are laying the blame at the feet of both the Liberal and Labor parties, saying our inaction on climate change is what's caused the conditions that led to the blazes. Firstly, to lump us in with Labor on anything is a low blow and instantly nullifies any argument you're trying to make, and second, the science on climate change is far from settled. I haven't done a lot of study in that area myself, but from what I know about scientific research, you can't just propose an idea that hasn't been proven yet. Further to that, the things that are currently making the most fire, aside from houses and animals, are trees – the same trees that the Greens are always saying are so beneficial to the environment. I'm also not seeing a lot of fires being put out by wind turbines.

What I have seen being used, to great effect, is petrol-fuelled jumbo jets dumping massive amounts of water on the flames and, yes, creating those emissions that are supposedly so detrimental to the planet. Fire trucks, too, burn petrol and create CO_2, which is exactly what those trees that the greenies love so much use for *food*. It only takes a small amount of critical thinking to realise that climate policies proposed by parties like the Greens just go around in circles and don't stand up to logic.

November 14ᵗʰ 2019

A group of former fire chiefs is saying they tried to warn
me about this bushfire season but that I knocked back
their meeting requests. Note the key word in that sentence
is 'former'. Why would I meet with someone not in the
job anymore? If I want to talk to an expert on computers,
I wouldn't set up a meeting with someone at the top of the
tech industry in the '90s, like Bill Gates. I'd want to meet
with someone who could tell me about the computers of
today, like Steve Jobs. They're trying to say that they told me
to bring in more water-bombers from the US, but how could
they have told me this if I didn't meet with them? As Donald
says, this is just more fake news. It should also be pointed
out that they're currently having a go at a guy who has given
nothing but his best thoughts and prayers during this crisis
and is currently working on a drought relief program. And
what would help prevent bushfires? If the drought ended!

November 18ᵗʰ 2019

China has knocked back a visa request for two of my
colleagues, James Paterson and Andrew Hastie, to speak
on human rights. Normally I'd understand a country not
wanting to let Paterson in, since he looks like a real estate
agent for mice, but the official reason they've given is
that the two of them had been critical of their country's

government. I heard from a source, though, that it's actually just because they're upset that we've been doing our own burning instead of exporting all the trees, houses and wildlife for them to do it.

November 21st 2019

It's pretty tough to breathe today, with all the smoke that has blown over Sydney. If this is what the summer is going to be like, I'm glad I'll be spending some of it in Hawaii.

November 23rd 2019

A man whose house burned down in the bushfires has spray-painted the remains with insulting messages to me, and I think it's in very poor taste. I don't take it personally, because he's obviously very upset that his home is gone, but I don't think it's appropriate to write 'F.U. Scomo' on the smoking remains of someone's house, even if it's your own. Politics has no place in a natural disaster. I did appreciate his acknowledgement of all of my thoughts and prayers, though. I've been thinking and praying perhaps harder than I ever have during this time, so it's nice to know people have noticed.

November 25th 2019

Here we go. Two weeks of sitting and then I don't have to work again until February. Eight days might seem like a long stretch of time to be constantly working, but I have to get my union-busting bill through and repeal the medevac legislation, so I'll have very little chance to relax.

November 26th 2019

Sometimes I feel like Labor will use any opportunity to have a dig at me. They've been ramping up their attacks on Angus Taylor since he's being investigated by the police after their referral, so I simply made a quick call to the police commissioner to have a chat about it and all hell has broken loose. They're saying I was trying to influence the case and that Angus should be stood down, which I've refused to do. Angus is innocent until proven guilty, regardless of whether he actually did it or not, and I will not punish an innocent man by preventing him from helping to vote through our unions bill and repeal of the medevac legislation.

November 27th 2019

I've had to do a lot of negotiating today. My union bill will hinge on the support of One Nation, so my first stop of the day was an early meeting with Pauline Hanson. Malcolm

Roberts was also there, but he had to stay tied up outside the café. I had my favourite breakfast – a plate of just bacon – and Pauline ordered her usual chicken parmy with BBQ sauce instead of tomato. She said she was a bit reluctant to help us with our numbers in the senate because some of her voters are working class, but I reminded her that a lot of unions also have Asians in them, which seemed to bring her around. I left feeling very good about our meeting, but that may have just been the bacon making me happy.

Next up I had to meet with Jacqui Lambie, who we need for our medevac repeal. Pauline is already completely on board with that one, for obvious reasons, but Jacqui has been going on about how she 'has a soul' and that it upsets her to see 'innocent people denied proper medical treatment'. She did, however, propose one thing that could get her to vote with us, something that we could never tell anyone about. The cost of this would be so great that I don't know if I am willing to give it to her, even if it means losing the vote. I will have to think long and hard on her offer.

November 28th 2019

That red-headed snake! I knew Lambie was against us from the beginning because she's a bogan, and if there's one thing they love more than swearing, it's unions, but Pauline was meant to be on our side! We are a nation built by

"Malcolm Roberts was also there, but he had to stay tied up outside the café.."

immigrants, so it would stand to reason that she'd be against builders. Reason and Pauline Hanson are obviously not well acquainted, though, and after putting forward eleven amendments to our bill, she turned around and stabbed us in the back by siding with Labor and the Greens. All we needed was one measly vote to get it over the line. Mathias told me he tried to lure Malcolm Roberts away with a liver treat, but Pauline had him on a choker chain, the poor creature.

I refuse to own this failure. This is a failure by Pauline to give the people of Australia what they want, so she's the loser here, not me. That said, I really need to get the medevac bill repealed now or I'm going to look like a complete twerp.

November 30th 2019

I was going to do a surprise bill if I got both of my other bits of work done early in these last two sitting weeks and introduce my religious discrimination legislation, but now Pauline's ruined all that. She's only hurt herself, though – it was worded to classify the burning of crosses as a protected form of religious expression. Well, that's all going to change when I introduce it next year now, and she's only got herself to blame.

December 3ʳᵈ 2019

God I'm smart. Those former fire chiefs have still been at me for a meeting about the bushfires, which feel like they'll never go out. Most people would expect me to take the normal route for a leader and just incessantly duck their requests until they either give up or the press get tired of interviewing them, but I am not a normal leader. Instead, I came up with an ingenious plan to kill two birds with one stone.

Obviously I'm too busy and they're too boring for me to want to meet with them myself, but by having Angus Taylor talk to them, not only do we give the impression that the government is listening and taking action, we also effectively clean any dirty laundry Angus may or may not have wrapped around the skeletons in his cupboard. If Albo continues to attack him now, he'll be asking for the resignation of the only man in the government who has spoken to a group of 'experts' on the bushfire crisis. We're effectively forcing Labor to choose between pursuing alleged corruption in the government and ensuring the wellbeing of Australian citizens. Given the level of corruption people have come to accept in this country, only one of those options is politically sensible. Checkmate, Albanese.

December 4ᵗʰ 2019

I've had to make a deal with the Tasmanian devil to get the medevac bill repealed. After Pauline screwed me over on my union legislation, I needed to get this one done. I couldn't let these past two weeks of backbreaking work have been for nothing, so I gave Jacqui what she wanted and we finally got medical evacuations for asylum seekers taken off the table for good.

I weighed up both sides of the argument and it will come at a cost to the government, but the ends justify the means and sometimes politics requires a compromise. I think both she and I come out of this ahead though. I finish my working year with a political victory and Jacqui gets a special card that gives her free Cokes from the Parliament House vending machine. Everybody wins. Well, everybody except asylum seekers, but that was kind of the point.

December 5ᵗʰ 2019

Today was a bit of a quiet one. It was the last day of parliament for the year, so we just took it easy and did a few Dorothy Dixers and a bit of jeering. I also bashed through my union bill in the lower house to get ready for next February when I can try to get it through the senate again. Hopefully Pauline will have come to her senses by then, or I can trade the reintroduction of the White Australia policy or something for her vote. More importantly, I am finally finished work! My big Hawaiian holiday is almost here!

December 7ᵗʰ 2019

Five fires have merged north of Sydney, creating one really big fire. My biggest thoughts and prayers go out to Gladys, who will have to deal with what is probably the most catastrophic state issue she's faced during her time in office so far. A section of the press are still talking about climate change, but what more do they want me to do? With our Kyoto credits, we are smashing our emissions targets. If anything, it's proof that climate change isn't man-made – we met our targets and we're *still* suffering through massive bushfires. If the fires are going to hit us anyway, then we may as well use that money we're wasting on emissions reduction to support the economy by digging up more coal. If my house burned down, something that would make

"...we just took it easy and did a few Dorothy Dixers and a bit of jeering."

me feel better is knowing I'd have a job down a mine and a lower energy bill when it was rebuilt, and only coal can provide those things.

December 8th 2019

Finally, a little bit of good news amongst all the carnage and horror of this bushfire season. Today I recorded my second improved Newspoll in a row, and although I'm sitting one point below where I was just after the election, we're still beating Labor 52 to 48, meaning that even though that yawning anus Albo defeated my union-busting bill, the people of Australia still despise him and love me, which is the real competition.

I was in such a good mood after seeing these results that I decided to help Gladys out with a bit of star power and visited the RFS command centre to get some pictures that she could put in the newspaper. State issues like these can be very trying for the premiers, so knowing that the Prime Minster is not only thinking and praying for them, but also willing to pay a visit to check up on everything, is incredibly helpful. I don't want to toot my own horn, but when it comes to tragedies, I'm not sure there's ever been a PM as thoughtful and prayerful as I am.

December 11th 2019

The air quality in Sydney today is dreadful. The city is blanketed in smoke and the experts have warned people that if they absolutely must go outside, they should try to avoid breathing. They've said that Sydneysiders are effectively smoking a pack of cigarettes a week just by being alive, so it's a shame they found that link between tobacco and cancer, because back in the '50s we could have sold the bushfires as a health product.

December 13th 2019

Boris just won the British election, and good on him. It's not every day that a man who looks like a pile of old clothes outside of an op-shop can unite a country and have them rally around severing crucial tradelines, but Boris has done it! This is a lesson to all of us to stick to your beliefs and don't back down for anyone. Sure, the UK might run out of food and, yes, he refuses to get a haircut because he's 'scared it will hurt', but he still won. In the end, that's all people will remember when he most likely dies from sticking a fork in a toaster. I sent out a little message to him on Tweeter, congratulating him and talking about the 'quiet Britons' to remind him who set the precedent for 'miracle' wins and who probably deserves at least half of the credit.

December 14th 2019

Gave myself a little pre-holiday break from all the talk of
fire and climate change tonight and took Jenny to see Tina
Arena at a new theatre in Rooty Hill. She must have known
I was in the audience because when she started to sing her
hit song 'Burn', it was like she was singing it just for me.
I will burn for you, Tina. I will burn for all Australians.
Just as soon as I get back from my holiday.

December 16th 2019

Hawaii! Finally! I've been looking forward to this for
so long, and after a week of breathing in smoke it feels
even better than expected. The skies are clear, the beer
is cold, and I'm ready for the best holiday of my life. I've
left my deputy, Patrick – or Phil, or something with a
P – in charge while I'm gone, but there's nothing really
happening on a federal level at the moment, so it's not
like he can mess up too much. I've decided to have what
they call a 'digital detox' while I'm there. I'll still use my
phone for playing games and watching funny videos on
YouTube, but I'm staying off Tweeter and avoiding the
news. This is my first holiday in almost six months, so
I need to fully enjoy it.

December 17th 2019

Today I sat by the pool, which just happens to also be by the beach, and drank a traditional local beverage created by the indigenous people. The Blue Hawaiian is made from rum, coconut, pineapple and a special ingredient known by the natives as blue curaçao. Normally I don't like foreign food, but this drink was so delicious that I polished off ten without even blinking. After my Blue Hawaiians, I tried to go for a swim but the lifeguard pulled me out because I hadn't come up for air for five minutes: 'I thought you were dead.' I shot back with, 'I was dead – dead relaxed from this wonderful island!' He high-fived me and had a waiter bring over another one of those special drinks but said the pool was closed to me until tomorrow.

Got a few texts from my deputy, I feel like it's Harrison or Mackenzie, but I deleted them without reading. He knows I'm on holiday. If it's really urgent he can call.

December 18th 2019

I got into an argument with a man at the breakfast buffet this morning. He was upset that, in making my usual plate of just bacon, I hadn't left much for the rest of the people in line. I told him that it sounded like he wasn't angry with me but with the kitchen, who clearly hadn't cooked enough. He asked if he could just have two pieces off my plate, so at least his wife could have some, but I was pretty sure that went against hygiene rules for food service, so I had to tell him no. Jenny and the girls also wanted some of my bacon when I got back to our table, but I told them that the rules don't just stop applying because we're related.

I've had a number of missed calls from my deputy, who I'm now seventy per cent sure is called Simon, but I won't be returning them. Being the Prime Minister is a full-time job, and I understand that I have to be on call 24/7, but not while I'm on holiday. I made him acting PM for a reason, so if he has any questions he can act like the leader he's meant to be standing in for and ask the people who tell me what to do.

December 19th 2019

That man from the buffet yesterday must have gotten there early today, because when I arrived for breakfast he was already at the front of the line. He looked me in the eye and took every last piece of bacon from the bain-marie. He thought he'd got one over on me, but I had a trick up my sleeve. I went and told the hotel manager what he'd done and got him in trouble and while they were screaming at each other, I snuck off with his plate. Jenny and the girls asked for some bacon again, but I reminded them that even though someone else had originally loaded the plate up, it was still against health and safety rules for me to share.

My deputy blew up my phone all day again. Every time I tried to play one of my games, the word 'Deputy' would flash up on the screen and I'd have to reject the call before I could get back to playing. It was so irritating that finally, about two hours after dinner, I picked up to tell him to go away. He told me that the bushfires still haven't gone out and that everyone is angry at me for going on holiday.

What kind of person, having seen how hard I've worked this year, would get mad about me taking a holiday after parliament finished until February? Especially when I haven't had one for *six whole months*! My deputy, Roger, or, I don't think it's Rohan, but I feel like it's similar, said that everyone wants me to go home early, but what would I do? Bushfires are a state issue and I'm not a premier. Does he expect me to hold the hose? I'm the Prime Minister, I don't hold the hose, mate! I told John, Paul, George or Ringo to leave me alone and that Australia will just have to deal with it. I'll be home on the 23rd – when I planned to be – then after Christmas and New Year's are out of the way I'll go and do as many photo ops as they want. Until then, I'm staying put.

December 20th 2019

I've been betrayed. My deputy and a few of my staffers drafted up a statement from me while I was asleep and released it to the press. I was happy that they said I'd been receiving regular briefings to get people off my back, but they ended it by saying that I'd be returning to Australia as soon as it could be arranged. My hand has been forced. I'll have to go home early, but I asked if they'd at least let me book the tickets so I could choose my airline. They agreed and I booked my flight for tomorrow morning, giving me one last day to drink beers by the pool. I think this whole thing has been blown out of proportion anyway. I met some Australians the other day who were thrilled to see me. They taught me how to do a Hawaiian thumbs-up, where you stick your pinkie out, and even asked for a photo. The public can't be that mad if they still love me enough to want a picture.

The buffet man was there again this morning. He'd lined up early, but this time he was with his wife and three children, and the five of them took all the bacon between them. I couldn't get the manager to tell him off again because they'd all only taken a relatively small amount each, so instead I said he'd threatened Jenny and the girls. His family have been asked to leave the resort.

December 21st 2019

After three days I was finally able to enjoy my bacon without any competition. It was a bittersweet victory though, because now I have to fly straight back into a political and literal firestorm. Even less fair, Jenny and the girls get to stay here for one more day, like we intended. After all the thoughts and prayers I so generously gave, the people of Australia have decided to ruin my holiday. I remembered that losing-a-day thing happens in Hawaii too, so I've told my office to tell any reporters waiting for me at the airport right now that I left through the back door and I'll sneak out when I get home.

December 22nd 2019

Went to a fire station today. It was boring. Not one person offered to bring me a cocktail and all they had to drink was water, not even any cordial. This sucks. I can't believe the Australian people wanted me to come home for this.

December 23rd 2019

Turns out people really do expect me to be out there, I just didn't understand the reason. They want me to act as a sort of coach for the state leaders. That's fine – I am technically their boss – but it would be nice if they could have handled things themselves, because at the moment I'm the one copping it for their failures. I understand that people are upset, so they're taking it out on the guy at the top. I just need to remind myself not to ever take it personally. Even though it's not my fault and, deep down, they're not really angry at me, I needed to clean up my image a bit in case Uncle Rupert rings some people who mistakenly blame me while he's doing next month's Newspoll. I decided to take a leaf out of Pauline's book after she got out of jail. I heard from *Dancing with the Stars* that they'd already cast the next season, so I skipped that step and just did the breakfast television part. As usual, the hosts of *Today* and *Sunrise* and their lady sidekicks were very nice to me, so by lunchtime I was back to my usual, high level of popularity.

December 24th 2019

Donald sent me some of his firefighters as a Christmas present. He's such a great guy. I think we'll be very close friends after we both move back to the private sector and don't have to be stuck at home all the time because a bunch of premiers can't put out a few fires. Canada also sent some firemen, but I assume that's only because that coiffured little prince didn't want to be left out.

December 25th 2019

Christmas had to be a bit more subdued this year. I still got my presents and ate and drank a lot, but I had to act like I wasn't enjoying it as much, in case someone took a picture of me smiling and Labor used it to smear me. I didn't have much of a chance to do any shopping because of my holiday and subsequent tour of fire stations, so for Jenny's gift I let her say some words at the start and end of my Christmas message to the people of Australia. I reckon she loved it because she was on the phone to her friends for half the day talking about it and crying tears of gratitude. I can't wait to wake up tomorrow and get stuck into the leftovers.

December 28th 2019

Albo is calling for the government to pay volunteer firefighters who have left their homes to battle the fires. It's like he doesn't know what the word volunteer means. If we paid them, they would just be regular firefighters, and we already have a lot of those.

December 29th 2019

Now the lefties are trying to cancel the New Year's Eve fireworks in Sydney. Leaving aside that the fireworks will probably be harder to see through all the smoke, what good does letting down an entire city do? Are they expecting the tears of all the disappointed children to put the fires out? This is just further proof to me that the PC police are also the fun police. They won't be happy until everyone is as miserable as them.

Well I, for one, am not miserable. I found out today that they're calling the bushfires The Morrison Fires, because of the brave leader who is going to put them out. This tells me that my morning on breakfast television talking to David Koch has worked, and the people now see me as the hero who cut his holiday short when he didn't have to, rather than a man who drank cocktails while Australia burned. The narrative has been reframed and once my mini-break covering the Christmas and

New Year's period is over, I'm going to get straight to the task of leading them into what will be Australia's most prosperous year: 2020.

January 1st 2020

2020! The year that will bring nothing but good fortune to Australia. Last night I hosted a party at Kirribilli House where my friends and I celebrated the fireworks not being cancelled by watching and enjoying them. With all that done, though, and after taking today off because it's a public holiday, it's now time to get to work doing what I do best: making ads. Tomorrow I'm going to travel to bushfire affected communities to get some footage of me listening to people and giving them comfort. We'll use this campaign to show Australians that I'm here for them, and we're going to get through this. The main message will be, 'These people have lost their houses, but look! They got to meet the Prime Minister! It's not all bad!' It has the potential to be my most successful commercial yet and really drive home just how much I care. People were a bit upset about how much we paid that empathy consultant, but after watching this ad I think they'll see that he was worth every cent.

January 2nd 2020

I get that people are sad right now, and I don't take it personally, but I wish the people in these burned-out towns were better on-screen talent. I only needed a few quick grabs, so we can cut around it, but with one woman I actually had to pick up her hand for the handshake so we could get the shot. Useless!

Once I had enough footage of me comforting civilians, we headed over to get some of me talking to the men on the front lines, the firefighters themselves. Not literally on the front lines, of course – that would be far too dangerous – but we went to their base to find some who were having a rest. I had to pick up another man's hand for a handshake while we were in the tent, but at least he had an excuse. He was obviously very tired from holding a hose, so I didn't mind helping him out and doing the heavy lifting in the exchange. He said something to me but I wasn't really listening because my head was full of camera angles and working out what we still needed for the ad. If it's not something that relates to our message, we can just drop the audio and put some music over it.

January 3rd 2020

I was supposed to be heading to India soon, but considering what happened the last time I got on a plane, I think it's probably best if I stay here for the moment. I was only going over there to sell them Australia's coal anyway, and I'm sure that can still be done over the phone.

January 4th 2020

My ad is a hit! I put it up on Tweeter today and it's had ten thousand comments and almost a hundred likes! I was really proud of my team when I saw it; they've even saved a bunch of money by using the hold music from one of the tax department's call centres. We weren't able to use any of the handshake footage because it was a bit too brief, but we did use some shots of me listening to people and surveying the damage from the same day, so the trip out to the country wasn't a complete waste of time.

January 5th 2020

I'm amazed at how vulgar the media can be sometimes.
All evening they've been playing a clip of a man telling me to
'get f**ked' and acting like he's some sort of working-class
hero. I don't take the insult personally – he's probably
delirious from heatstroke – but to play that on the news,
where impressionable children could see it and think it's
how Australians really feel, is despicable.

January 6th 2020

I've just announced a $2 billion fund to help with bushfire
relief. I'm a bit concerned about what it's going to do to our
surplus, but I reckon if we can sell a bit more coal to India
and China, we should be able to make up the difference.

January 7th 2020

Donald just called to offer his own thoughts and prayers
in this difficult time, which surprised me as I didn't know
he had thoughts and he's told me a number of times that
he doesn't see the point of praying because if he needs to
talk to God he can just look in the mirror. I asked if I could
maybe have some of that moon money back, to help out
with my budget, and the line went dead. America is the
greatest country in the world, but their infrastructure

isn't the best . . . I did post on Tweeter tagging him in so everyone knows we're mates. Hopefully he sees that and calls back with an answer when his phone starts working again.

January 9th 2020

Some members of the press are trying to smear me again. I visited Kangaroo Island today and made a comment that it was good that no one had died. A lady said that two people from the community had, and I clarified that I had been talking about firefighters. That should have been that, but all of a sudden there are headlines about me being 'embarrassed' and 'red-faced', when I am nothing of the sort. Why would I be? It wasn't *me* who misunderstood my first comment – it was the lady I was talking to. If anyone was embarrassed it was her. I think the real tragedy of this whole bushfire season has been how low journalistic standards have fallen.

January 10th 2020

Today saw widespread protests across the country calling for me to be sacked. I don't take it personally because lefties are incapable of rational thought, and anyone else in that crowd is just taking their anger about the fires out on me, but to politicise a tragedy like this is sick. It's a shame I wasn't able to outlaw protesting last year, because if I pass that legislation now it will look like I'm only doing it because they're against me, but I must remember to have my people draft up a bill that I can put through when all of this is over in March. I can't imagine there will be much happening in Australia by then.

January 12th 2020

I had a brilliant idea today! I've proposed a royal commission into the bushfires. Through this, I will end up with a report that clearly states that this was an issue for the premiers and that I should never have been forced to cut my holiday short. This morning's Newspoll showed our party trailing Labor for the first time since the election, but I can spot one of Uncle Rupert's tests from a mile off now. If he only printed that our party was behind Labor, then I might have been fooled, but he had my personal rating behind Anthony Albanese's. It's just so obvious. There is no way in a million years that anyone could believe that I am less popular than Albo, a man who sounds like someone farting into a vacuum cleaner.

January 17th 2020

I've got a new nickname! People all over Facebook have been calling me Scotty from Marketing, and honestly? I kind of love it. I've always wanted people to call me Scotty. I tried to get my friends and family to use that name when I was a boy, but I was told people aren't allowed to choose their own nicknames. The marketing bit just tops it off. Finally, I am being recognised for what I do best.

Scotty from Marketing sounds like the coolest guy at the party, the one everyone sits around talking about before he arrives, then when he walks through the door they go, 'Quiet, he's here,' because they don't want to embarrass him

NICKNAME
SHORTLIST

Scotty M.
The M-Man
M-Dog
M-Dawg
ScoMo   scoMO
SCOMO!   SCOmo
S.Mo S+M
Scott, Heaps of Mates
Scoomie Doo
S.Mores
The Morry Lorry

with all their praise. Scotty from Marketing sounds exactly like the person I am. I also love it because it can't be turned into anything mean for a joke. Scomo is fine, but I've been getting a little bit sick of everyone in Parliament House calling me Scummo, even if that kind of gentle teasing is just a sign of how much everyone likes me.

January 20th 2020

I've just been made aware that the 'Scotty from Marketing' thing isn't a compliment. It's an insult from the Tweeter lefties of the Labor Party, probably the same ones who think it's square to wear shoes. The communist pricks. What kind of person thinks marketing, one of the world's oldest and most noble professions, is an insult? I spin things and sell the great work the government is doing because it makes people feel good. I mean, imagine the panic I'd cause if I came out and said, 'The world is on fire, Australia is barrelling towards being an uninhabitable hellscape, and there's nothing we can do about it.' When you see a bunch of shirtless youths on television, abs rippling, downing bottle after bottle of full-sugar Coke, you feel good about the fact you'd rather drink gallons of black acid a day in place of water. If those ads instead showed an obese man struggling to walk up a flight of stairs or having a root canal, you'd feel far more anxious. Marketing, much like religion, is an act of mercy. People put their faith in a higher power, and in doing so, absolve themselves of all worry and doubt. Without ad men to repackage the truth, the world would be a much scarier place.

January 21st 2020

My deputy's deputy, Bridget McKenzie, is in trouble at the moment over her sports grant bribes before the election. A report came out about a week ago and it's really starting to pick up steam. Honestly, this could not have come at a better time for me – this is exactly why we formed the Coalition in the first place, so that the Liberals would always have someone crazier to take the heat during a scandal. I'm fairly sure there's a loophole that makes what she did with the grants technically legal, but either way, the longer I can keep her in a job, the more the cries for her to resign will drown out anything to do with me and the fires. What a gift.

January 25th 2020

People are upset that we've decided to give Bettina Arndt an Australia Day award for services to gender equality. It's typical for the outrage brigade to not understand the basic meaning of words, but 'equality' means the same rights for everyone, not just those on the Left. You can't dismiss the things Arndt says just because they hold no factual weight – you have to give equal attention to all sides of an argument. That means that people who hate women should have their voice heard just as much as the feminists; everyone should be allowed to call themselves a doctor, regardless of whether or not they hold a PhD; and a person who deserves an Australia Day honour should have no more chance of receiving one than someone like Bettina.

January 26th 2020

Thank God for Australia Day. In these fractured times, with the country divided by protests and natural disasters, it's good to know that the one thing that everyone can agree on is our national day. A day that celebrates those core Australian values of mateship, a fair go and printing the flag onto a paper plate and eating burnt chops off it.

January 29th 2020

Today I have to deliver my first speech to the National Press Club for the year, and it's the perfect opportunity to ram home just how great our government is. People are getting tired of hearing about the bushfires at this point and are practically begging for some good news, so I spent the whole speech talking about the strength of the economy, our world-leading climate change policy and how what people have been calling 'sports rorts' were actually much-needed grants used, among other things, to build female change rooms. Now if by chance a woman plays at one of these men's sporting clubs, she will no longer have to hypothetically change in the middle of the field. The narrative has, once again, been reframed, and I think my speech will bring a lot of comfort to the people who voted for us.

January 31st 2020

Some new virus has sprung up in China and a few people have reportedly brought it back here. I've made a rule that any foreign national has to spend two weeks in a different country first if they're coming in from China. This way they can infect people somewhere other than Australia, and the only sick people we'll get will be Australians, who have fantastic immune systems and access to Medicare. It's the perfect plan to keep the country healthy and, more importantly, open for business.

February 2nd 2020

I actually don't know what Uncle Rupert wants from me at this point. Jesus only got tested once in the Bible, so why am I seeing these negative Newspolls for a second time? I don't have an election to win and I've effectively shifted attention from the bushfires onto Bridget McKenzie, who unfortunately had to resign as my deputy deputy today over her role in the sports rorts affair. His surveys should be singing my praises, but instead he's saying I'm only as popular as Albo was two months ago. That pumpkin in a toupee is now, on paper, more popular than me. I don't take it personally, because it's not true, but it is a little insulting.

February 3rd 2020

Michael! My deputy's name is Michael! I would never have guessed that . . . Anyway, I might not need to know his name after tomorrow – Barnaby just announced he's going to stand against him in a spill.

February 4th 2020

Turns out Barnaby's ex-wife was right: he is a loser. My deputy, and his name completely escapes me again, remains my deputy, and his new deputy is David Littleproud, a man who, if I had to think of a way to describe him, is a person with a face.

February 5th 2020

It's not often I'll say this, but Peter Dutton did pretty
well today. He's figured out a clever way of reframing the
narrative around bushfires and climate change. Instead of
talking about the conditions that caused the fires to spiral
out of control, he's placing all the blame at the feet of the
arsonists who started them. After all, it wasn't the climate
that lit the match, it was a person – a person we can vilify.
Australians respond very well to hate. It's the reason TV
shows like *Getting Married at First Sight* and the cooking
show hosted by that irradiated wellness skeleton rate so
highly, so giving them a human target other than me to aim
their anger at is a genius idea.

I'm also giving the public a second target in the Greens,
because if there weren't any trees, there wouldn't have been

any fuel. I reckon there's probably a good amount of jobs in the complete deforestation of Australia too, so we should be able to kill all the birds with one stone and get our unemployment figures down at the same time.

February 6th 2020

The AFP have decided that there's not enough evidence to proceed with an investigation into Angus Taylor's documents, and rightly so. Angus is a very experienced politician. Now the federal police can get back to going after the real criminals – journalists who gain access to sensitive information and use it to embarrass the government.

February 11th 2020

It feels pretty ironic that it's just rained so much in Sydney that the city has been hit by floods. I suppose the lefty hordes will try to blame this one on climate change as well, but how can it be responsible for bushfires and floods at the same time? Fire and water are literally the exact opposite of each other.

Today in parliament, Bill Shorten, who is still alive apparently, called for $1.5 billion of budget surplus we raised with our robodebt system to be returned because collecting it was 'illegal'. If it was so illegal, then why did

people pay it back? The only reason he wants me to return it is because he's jealous that my surplus is going to be massive and the only time a Shorten ever delivered anything that big was Bill's mother when she gave birth to his head.

February 13th 2020

About forty people on a cruise ship in Japan have tested positive for that virus from China. It's not much to be worried about, since it's still only in Asia, but I've extended our rule where you have to go somewhere else before coming here from China for another week or so, just in case.

February 17th 2020

After all the subsidies I gave them, General Motors have decided to close down Holden in Australia, meaning people living in the outer suburbs will no longer have to pry the badges off their cars to replace them with the American version. On the bright side, we should be able to spin this in a few months to highlight a shift away from petrol-burning vehicles.

February 19th 2020

Turns out that fireman who said those rude things about me is a One Nation voter and the lefties are having an aneurism. Now, in order to avoid being called racist, they're forced to condemn a man who told me to 'get f**ked', and in doing so, end up supporting me. It's not often in politics that you achieve a checkmate this perfect, so when one comes along it's something to be savoured. It feels good to win.

February 21st 2020

China is having a real problem with this virus of theirs. I feel a bit bad for them. There are still a handful of cases in Australia, but nothing like over there. A few people have asked me what I'd do if we ended up with an epidemic, or worse, a pandemic, but I don't think that's going to happen.

Something like that would be the making of a great leader, but according to the quote, 'Some are born great, some achieve greatness, and some have greatness thrust upon them.' I was born great, so God would have no reason to thrust upon me. No, I'm fairly sure this whole thing will blow over soon and we can get back to flying in wealthy Chinese nationals to gamble in our casinos.

February 22nd 2020

Albo just went on *Insiders* and said he expects Australia to still be exporting coal by 2050. While I agree with him, because digging up coal for people to burn is an excellent money-spinner, having Anthony as opposition leader is kind of taking the fun out of winning. If we imagine I'm the legendary boxer Rocky, it's like I've walked to the ring to find Mr T lying in the corner with no arms or legs. They've also changed the rules of boxing, so now all I have to do is kick him to death. I mean, I'm still Rocky, so the crowd is excited just to get to see me, but the fight itself is a little underwhelming, if I'm honest. It's just Sylvester Stallone (me) kicking a limbless torso, which, if the more recent Rambo films are anything to go by, isn't going to sell a lot of tickets.

A great hero needs a great villain to truly cement his legacy. A Moriarty to his Sherlock Holmes, a Caesar to his Brutus, a Betty to his Don Draper. Realistically, Labor is

"...it's like I've walked into the ring to find Mr. T lying in the corner with no arms or legs."

going to keep putting up leaders like Shorten and Albanese, and I'm going to continue to crush them at every election. The only real advice any future leader of this party needs from me at this point is to just let Labor be Labor. As such, I've decided to finish my diary here and send it off to be published. Let me make this clear – this decision has nothing to do with the fact that I have found out that they made more than one Angry Bird game and I'll have far less free time to commit to writing. I just think this is a logical end point.

If something big or interesting happens, or Labor finally gives me a worthy opponent, I might pick up my biro again and write a sequel (or, better yet, just knock off a couple of extra chapters for this book and rerelease it as a revised edition), but they show no signs of doing so. Hell, if Albo copies any more of my policies we might just roll his party into ours and create a super coalition, the LNLP. No more crossbench, no more elections, just an almighty juggernaut with me at the wheel, ploughing down anyone who stands in opposition to the Australian people: the real ones, the quiet ones. Kind of like America. I might have one of my guys pitch this to Albanese, actually . . .

My prediction is that nothing of note will happen in the world over the next few years, so this diary will now stand as a testament to my first eighteen months as Prime Minister and Chief Marketing Officer of the Australian Government

Pty Ltd. My hope is that it gives a brief insight into what it is like to achieve and maintain my levels of success. I am sure it will be beneficial to people from all walks of life – be they a CEO, an Olympic athlete or even just a humble junior marketing executive, dreaming of one day getting to make a pretty lady say a swearword on the telly.

Whoever you are, I want to leave you with one piece of advice: believe in yourself. Not everyone is made for the level of greatness I have achieved (I am, after all, a once-in-a-generation talent), but everyone is put on this earth for something, and there is nothing anyone can do to change that. When the chips are down, remind yourself that the world owes you. Work as much or as little as you want, schedule frequent breaks, and don't be afraid to take a holiday every couple of months. Nothing can stop you if you're meant for bigger things, so sit back, crack a beer and let life drag you towards your destiny.

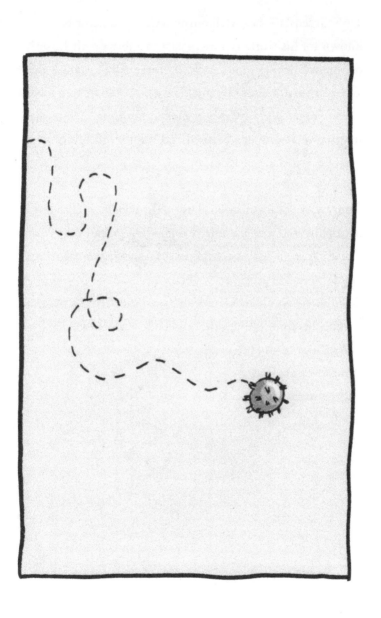

Tosh Greenslade is a Melbourne writer and actor best known for his work as a main cast member on all 12 series of Shaun Micallef's *Mad as Hell* on the ABC. A graduate of The National Theatre Drama School, he has written for the *Good Food Guide* and performed at both the Melbourne International Comedy Festival and Edinburgh Fringe Festival. @toshgreenslade

Andrew Weldon's cartoons have been widely published nationally and internationally, including in the *New Yorker*, *Private Eye*, the Chaser publications, the *Sydney Morning Herald* and *The Age*. He has been a cartoonist for the *Big Issue Australia* since its inception in 1996. He has published book collections of his work and children's books. He lives in Melbourne and he smells funny.
@aweldoncartoons,
andrewweldon.com